Calligraphy for Greetings Cards and Scrapbooking

PETER E. TAYLOR

First published 2012 by
Guild of Master Craftsman Publications Ltd
Castle Place, 166 High Street, Lewes,
East Sussex BN7 1XU

Reprinted 2013

ISBN: 978-1-86108-882-6

A catalogue record for this book is available from the British Library.

Publisher: Jonathan Bailey
Production Manager: Jim Bulley
Managing Editor: Gerrie Purcell
Project Editor: Gill Parris
Managing Art Editor: Gilda Pacitti
Designers: Rebecca Mothersole/Rob Janes
Photography: Peter E. Taylor, all step-by-step photographs, and finished item
    photographs, unless otherwise stated.
Illustrations: Peter E. Taylor

Set in ITC Century BT, Bodoni Hand, Kalligraf Latin and Sketch Script.
Colour origination by GMC Reprographics
Printed and bound in China

CONTENTS

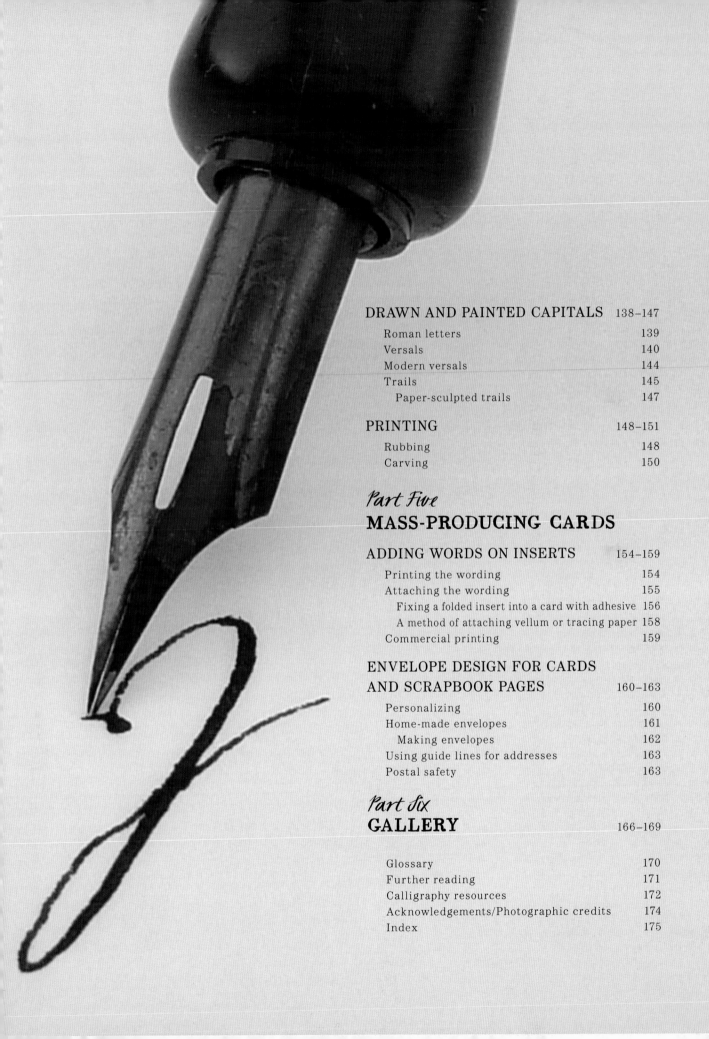

Introduction

When an original greetings card is made especially for someone, or a personal message is written by hand inside a card, the recipient will feel the emotion that the sender wishes to express. This is conveyed by the choice of words and reflected in the way that they are presented. Similarly, scrapbook pages are created to display a very personal interpretation of events and feelings.

Occasionally, mechanically produced words, layouts and backgrounds may suffice, but when used alone they can limit expression and creativity. In this book I show you how to add your own personality to your cards and scrapbook pages and to produce creations that are uniquely your own.

The techniques described and designs shown are not just for copying – although you are welcome to do that if you wish – but to be developed through experimentation and moulded to suit your personal vision for a finished artwork.

Calligraphy, as used here, is interpreted as 'the artistic design and use of hand-crafted letters', not just as 'beautiful handwriting'. Although handwriting can be calligraphic, calligraphy and handwriting are two separate skills. You do not need neat handwriting to create good calligraphy, indeed the shopping lists and diary notes of many professional scribes are often a mess. Even when producing lettering that looks joined like handwriting, a calligrapher will think of each letter as a drawing of what is visualized as the perfect shape, and its placement will be carefully considered.

As well as being used for evenly spaced and stylish writing, calligraphic letters can be carved on an eraser to make a printing block, written with a piece of broken balsa wood, painted as a single ornate and decorative letter, or embossed by raising the paper surface. Some calligraphy requires a pen with a square-cut chisel-shaped nib to be used, which automatically produces thick and thin letter strokes in the correct places. But not all calligraphy is 'thick and thin' and many letter designs can be drawn with a pencil, ballpoint pen, or other everyday writing implement.

Scrapbooking and card-making are enjoyable activities and the hours fly by when you are lost in a world of creativity. Likewise, when using calligraphy, enjoyment comes not only from the finished result, but also from expressing your own personality and feeling in the rhythms of writing. Letters can be modified, flourishes added, letter slope and emphasis varied, and a writing medium selected to best fit the chosen words and choice of papers – the possibilities are endless.

The tips and instructions provided come from many years of experience and enjoyment from calligraphy and paper-crafting. I hope you will have fun using the techniques described to produce your own unique, professional-looking cards and scrapbook pages.

How to Use this Book

The primary aim of this book is to help readers develop skills that enable them to draw well-shaped letters, to apply, arrange and space them effectively and creatively on cards and scrapbook pages – and to have fun whilst doing so.

The early sections show the methods, used by master scribes throughout the centuries, to consistently draw elegant letters and create layouts and designs that delight – techniques that should work for all who wish to learn calligraphy.

The letter styles can be used for many purposes and, if the instructions are followed carefully, a sound understanding of the principles of good calligraphy can be achieved. It is best to gain skill in drawing and using the letters of one or two alphabets, and to practise writing and applying them one by one, rather than attempting to learn every alphabet described here as soon as each is discovered.

You do not need to gain 'master calligrapher' status before using the later chapters in the book. A single decorated calligraphic letter or two may be all that is required for some projects and, whatever level of expertise you have, the ideas and tips throughout the book can be used at any time to add lettering to a project. Each card and page shows particular writing styles in use, and I hope these will inspire and encourage you to experiment and explore new possibilities.

While fluent writing in calligraphy does take practice, the wonderful thing is that wording for most scrapbooking and card-making will be short and can be written and perfected on paper or card that is then cut and attached to the final artwork. It is easy for anyone to learn to write beautiful individual letters calligraphically, apply them with almost immediate success, and then work up to longer and longer amounts of text and a wider variety of scripts.

PART ONE

Basics

Everyday Tools and Equipment

Special calligraphy pens are not needed to write in all calligraphy styles.
The letters of some alphabets can be drawn and decorated with anything
that is already to hand that will make a mark.

Graphite pencils, coloured pencils, pastels, ballpoint pens, felt or fibre-tip pens, paint and artists' brushes, sticks or even clothes pegs, can be used, so it is possible to start to learn the craft and easily produce attractive results before investing in specialist broad-edged writing tools or nibs. However, for cards and scrapbooking, almost certainly you will need the following calligraphy tools at some time soon after you start.

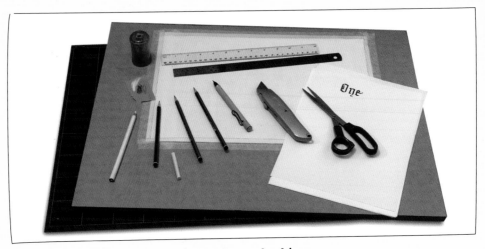

Basic equipment for card-making and scrapbooking.

2H, HB and 2B Pencils and Pencil Sharpeners
For creating the sharpest points, artists often use a very sharp knife, or push and twist the pencil as the lead is rubbed over fine sandpaper, as well as, or instead of, using a normal sharpener. Mechanical 'click pencils' with 0.35mm or 0.5mm leads are an excellent alternative. White coloured pencils are useful for lightly drawing guide lines on dark paper and card.

Eraser The soft white variety that is manufactured in long cylindrical shapes about ¼in (5mm) in diameter is an excellent choice. The tip of these can easily be introduced between letters to remove lines, reducing the danger of removing ink or colour from the writing. They can also be trimmed with a sharp knife so that they fit, when necessary, into even tighter places.

Craft Knife Choose one with a pointed, rigid and razor-sharp blade.

Rulers A clear plastic ruler for drawing guidelines. A metal ruler can also be used as a straight edge for trimming paper and card with a craft knife.

Self-healing Cutting Mat
This is a good investment, as it protects the surface underneath. Alternatively, solid thick cardboard can be used for cutting on. Cuts made on to cardboard will soon blunt blades, but probably not as quickly as those made on wood or laminate surfaces.

Paper For practice, the kind of paper sold for use in photocopiers and laser-printers is perfectly adequate. Thin 'layout paper', often sold in pads in art-supply stores, can be particularly useful because it is transparent enough to enable you to see pre-drawn guide lines on a sheet placed underneath, which saves time. Papers most suited for finished work are discussed on page 39.

Sharp Scissors For cutting out letter shapes and general paper-crafting.

Writing Board You can purchase custom-built drawing boards, but a piece of MDF (medium-density fibreboard), or a similar rigid wooden board about 1ft 4in x 2ft (40 x 60cm) and ½in (12mm) thick works well, too. If it has been machine cut for sale in a store, it will probably have sides that are accurately straight and at right angles to each other, useful for sliding a T-square along, if you wish.

T-Square (optional) If you have a board with straight, right-angled sides, a T-square can be helpful for ruling lines.

Light-box This device is exceptionally useful in helping to produce perfectly spaced lettering and fitting words into particular spaces – craftspeople often regard it as their most treasured aid. A light-box doesn't actually have to be box-shaped: the principle is that a light source is provided underneath a translucent top, and this backlight helps the calligrapher to see and trace pre-written lettering that is laid on it, on to other paper, or thin card. A light-box can be purchased, or home-made (see pages 14–15).

A guard sheet prevents the writing surface being affected by oil from the skin.

Purpose-built light-box

You can purchase commercially made and traditionally shaped light-boxes with sloping or flat tops which are excellent (below left), and manufacturers are also now producing wonderful energy-saving, slim devices based on a large LED panel (below right). The examples below are from Artograph.

A commercially manufactured light-box.

An LED-lit panel.

Low-cost alternatives

Alternatively, to save financial outlay and to achieve the same result as that obtained by using a box structure, a light source can simply be placed under a glass-topped coffee table, or between two chairs, with a piece of white acrylic rested on the seats (right). The acrylic should be sufficiently thick to ensure that it doesn't sag much when you rest your hand on it. A cold light source in an old drawer, with acrylic over the top, would also work well.

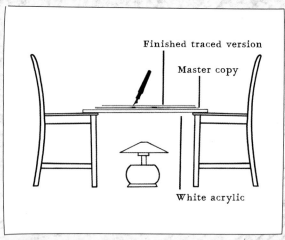

Finished traced version

Master copy

White acrylic

A low-cost alternative to a light-box.

 TO MAKE A
LIGHT-BOX

It is also possible to make a simple light-box that will work perfectly
satisfactorily for a large number of years.

YOU WILL NEED:
Base: ¾in (18mm) MDF or particle-board base

Sides: ⁷⁄₁₆ –½in (10–12mm) thick, smooth
dressed-pine, or MDF. Note: when standing on
the base, the sides must be high enough to hold the
acrylic sheet above the light source

Light source: 2 x 15 watt daylight coiled
fluorescent bulbs and holders, which won't
heat the surface, or a fluorescent strip light

Translucent top: ³⁄₁₆in (5mm) white acrylic
plastic sheeting

Flex and screws

1. Cut the base to be a rectangle about 14 x 18in
(35 x 45cm).

2. Measure the height the light source will stand
when it is mounted on the base of the light-box.
This will tell you how high the sides should
be – probably about 1in (2.5cm) higher after they
have been attached. The sides can be screwed
to the sides of the base or on top of it.

3. N.B. For safety, wiring should be done by a
qualified electrician. As the box will need to
be placed on a table for use, the flex should
enter from the side. Take your box and bulb
fittings to a tradesperson for completion.
They should provide a switch or tell you what
kind should be purchased, and install it. Inform
them that the top will not be fixed to the sides.

4. The top sheet of white acrylic plastic should
overlap the edges by about ½in (12mm), as it
is often useful to be able to move and swivel
it around without moving the box.

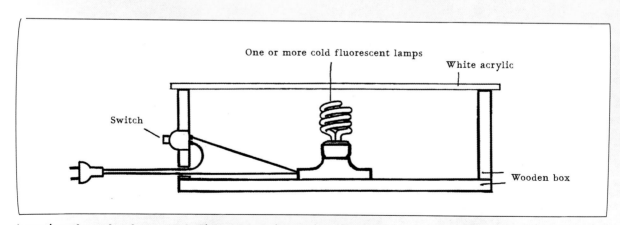

A section through a home-made light-box. This one is 14in L x 18in W x 3in H (35 x 45 x 10cm).

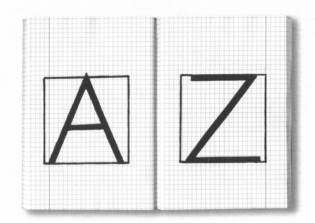

Letters We Rely On

The 'classic' letters first painted and carved by the Romans have determined the basic shapes, and relative proportions, of all capital letters in every Western writing style and type font developed since AD 100.

Roman Letters

A thorough understanding of the structure of these foundation letters is helpful when writing in modern styles that have been adapted from them, and also when designing or modifying letters ourselves. The easiest way to learn the special features of these Roman letters is initially to draw simplified 'skeleton' versions using a writing tool that produces a line of a constant thickness, for example, a pencil or fine fibre-tipped pen, and relating the letter shapes to a square (see facing page). For initial practice, graph paper with ¼in (5mm) squares is useful to write on – preferably in boxes four squares high and wide, but they can be written any size and soon should be written freehand.

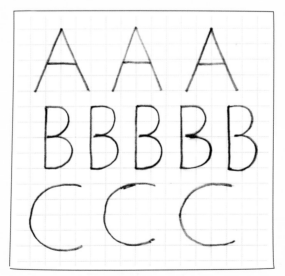

Graph paper with ¼in (5mm) squares is useful for practising the letter shapes.

SKELETON ROMAN CAPITALS

The shape of 'O' controls the shape of other letters

C D G O Q

These fit into a square

B E F I J K L P R S

These fit into half a square

A H N T U V

The letters in this line, and the first three letters of the
line below, fit into three-quarters of a square

X Y Z M W

M and W are wider than a square

The special features of these letters are shown overleaf.

The vertical of 'G' nearly reaches the midway line. Notice, too, that all the rounded letters have been drawn so that their top and bottom edges are just a fraction above and below the edges of the boxes.

The tops of 'C' and 'S' (and 'G') are slightly flattened, as is the bottom of 'S'.

The top bowl of the 'B' is smaller than the bottom.

The middle bar of 'E' sits on the mid-line, which runs through the lower bar of 'F'. The top of 'F' is wider than the top of 'E'. 'E' has a wider bottom than top and a middle bar only a fraction narrower.

The limbs of 'K' hit the vertical a fraction above the mid-line and the bottom is wider than the top.

The bowl of 'P' extends to just below the mid-line.

The diagonal of 'R' hits the bottom guide line to make the bottom wider than the top. The bowl of 'R' is a fraction lower than that of 'P'.

The bottom area of 'S' is bigger than that enclosed in the top. The top and bottom strokes of 'S' are nearly flat and parallel to each other.

The position of the bar of 'A' depends on the thickness of the strokes. Look at the distance created between the bottom guide line and the inside of the inverted 'V' shape at the top, and imagine this divided in two by a line. The bar will be drawn so the line runs through its centre.

The bar of 'H' sits on top of the mid-line.

The top of 'X' is narrower than the bottom and the crossing point is above the mid-line.

The top of 'Z' is narrower than the bottom.

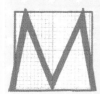

The most important thing with 'M' is to make the first and last angles the same.

The tip of 'A' and top pointed corners of 'N' (and 'M') protrude a tiny amount. This makes them look the same height as other letters.

B D P R E L

Optional added slopes to letters

There are many calligraphic writing styles with letters of different shapes but, for elegant appearances, it is still always safest to keep to these Roman features, such as the bar of 'H' sitting on top of the mid-line, 'K' and 'R' being widest at the bottom, and so on.

When you have practised these skeletal letter shapes for a while, you may then wish to make them slightly more complex by adding even more traditional features from the early carved Roman letters – sloping the tops of 'B', 'D', 'P' and 'R' upwards and the bottoms of 'B' and 'D' downwards a fraction. The bottoms of 'E' and 'L' can also be drawn as ogee curves, like an 'S' on its side that has been given an enormous stretch, but it is very easy to overdo this curve, so always aim to keep these strokes mainly straight, as shown above.

Colour added inside the letters does not touch the letter strokes.

SKELETON ROMAN SMALL LETTERS

These are a fraction bigger than 60% of the capital height – ideally the ratio is 4:6.5.

a b c d e f g g h
i j k l m n o p q r
s t u v w x y z

Just as the shapes of all Roman small letters are based on a square and a circle, as drawn here, so the small letters of any other alphabet will look well constructed if they relate to the size and shape of each other and have as many family resemblances as possible.

ABCDEFGHI
JKLMNO
PQRSTU
VWXYZ

Decorated versions of Roman
capitals. Be creative and
design your own, too.

SPLISH

Decorated skeleton
Roman letters mixed with
Italic. Another possibility
is to mix pens and draw
some letters or parts
of letters in a range of
colours and thicknesses.

SPLASH

The 23ct gold used in the hearts shines.
Using real gold for these little touches is
easy and not expensive (the technique
is explained on pages 132–137).

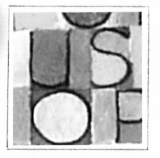

Here a waterproof
permanent marker
was used for the letters
first, then watercolour
paint added.

20

ABCDEFG
HIJKLMN
OPQRST
UVWXYZ

Here the rules of normal proportions of classic Roman capitals have been broken deliberately, with the letters heavily weighted at the top and bottom, so that it doesn't appear that mistakes have been made.

BEGINNER GARDENERS LEARN BY TROWEL & ERROR

As shown with this 'A' and 'L', apart from dramatically changing the positions of letter features, lines can be fractionally curved and first drawn lightly and simply in graphite or coloured pencil, then the writing tool carefully flicked back along these lines, with most pressure exerted at the extremities. This drawing technique can also be used on other alphabets.

A Place for Our Calligraphy

The simple and essential techniques described in this chapter will help to ensure that any finished product you create will look elegant and well finished.

Envelopes and Stamps

Some craft enthusiasts like simple, unadorned pages, cards and envelopes, while others prefer them to be complex and highly embellished. They also have personal tastes about the degree to which they want every element to coordinate or contrast.

It is a good idea to select your envelope before making a card, so that you know that colours will harmonize and that the card will fit comfortably inside it. If you want to use one made from a coloured or textured paper, the choice will be more limited, unless you make your own. (Instructions for making envelopes to suit your needs are given on pages 162–163.)

At an early stage, also consider what stamp will be attached, as this may affect the choice of colour for the envelope paper and also that of the card, any background you create, the ink or paint that you write with – and maybe other picture or design features.

Postal services prefer a clearer address than this, though it would get delivered eventually. Cards in very decorative envelopes can be given personally and sculptural cards sent in boxes.

The stamps used on this envelope inspired the colours and design of the background vegetation and animals on the envelope and card, which were drawn using coloured pencils.

Envelopes can also be used to title a scrapbook page or to signify the location where photographs were taken.

Finding the Grain of Paper and Card

The paper fibres in hand-made paper are arranged at random, allowing it to be folded easily in any direction. Machine-made card and paper, however, have a 'grain' that results from the pulp being poured on to a moving belt and the fibres tending to line up with the direction the belt is moving.

If a piece of your chosen machine-made card or paper – preferably close to square in shape – is bent gently without creasing it, it may be possible to detect that it bends more easily in one direction than the other, see {a} and {b}.

The direction of the grain of thin paper is sometimes hard to detect by this 'squeeze' method. One alternative is to try the 'pinch test', see {c} and {d}.

Greetings cards should always be made with the grain running along the fold, and scrapbook pages created with the grain running parallel to their vertical edge and the spine of the book.

Whenever layers of card and paper are attached to each other, the grain of each should run in the same direction. This is the golden rule of all paper-crafting because it minimizes buckling and bubble effects and allows for optimal ease of flexing. However, hand-made papers, with no grain, can be glued in any orientation to other papers.

If you still cannot detect which way the grain runs, cut a small square of the paper (marking or noting how this relates to the whole sheet). Moisten the surface of the small square with water, perhaps using a cloth or tissue. The paper square should start to curl. The grain runs parallel to the long side of the cylinder. All sheets of this particular paper or card that have the same dimensions will almost certainly have the grain running in the identical direction to that of the test piece.

If you need to score card to aid easy folding, the card should always be bent away from the dent that the blunt instrument has made, see {e} and {f}.

 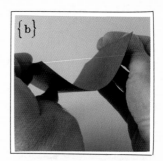

Equal pressure is applied to opposite sides of a sheet of paper or card. The grain runs parallel to the 'easy' fold.

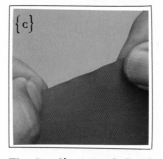 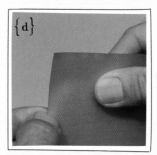

The forefinger and the thumbnail grip the paper edge, then first one edge is pulled and then the one at right angles to it. One edge should pucker more than the other. The grain runs parallel to the smoothest edge.

When scoring card to ease folding, bend the sides so that the depression stays on the outside of the crease.

CREATING PLATEMARKS

A border of some kind usually enhances words written on the front of cards and pages. One of the easiest ways of adding one that looks professional is to emboss a sunken 'platemark' in the surface. This can be accomplished before or after the words are written. This technique works best when the finished card or page is made out of thin card that has a warm feel, which means it has long paper fibres.

Template card on the front surface.

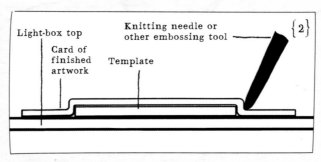

The finished card is bent around the template.

Embossing the platemark.

1. A piece of cardboard about shoebox thickness is cut to the size of the chosen platemark panel and laid on the front of the card or the page's top surface. While tightly holding the two together, the smaller platemark-creating embossing card is placed against a backlit window or light-box top, and the greetings card opened.

2. The rounded end of a thick knitting needle (about gauge 3–6), ball-ended embossing tool or similar object with a rounded tip, is gently drawn just to the outside of the embossing card to bend the greetings card or page card around its edge. This diagram shows a 'cross section' view.

3. For a crisp finish, the needle can then be drawn tighter to the edge, two or three more times, applying greater pressure.

The finished platemark.

Embossing dark card

If the card of the greetings card or scrapbook page is dark in colour, you cannot see where the embossing card is underneath, no matter how bright the backlight. It is then easiest to work on a horizontal flat board, or surface (not a valued table, which could get marked) and to use a thick knitting needle.

Find the edge of the platemark.

Sharpen the embossing.

Keeping the knitting needle parallel to the side of the embossing card and at a very shallow angle to the work surface, slide it on its side towards the embossing card to find the edge, and then rub gently to establish the outline {a}. The needle can then be used more vertically so that the point can sharpen the platemark {b}.

You don't have to limit yourself to large rectangular indentations. You could add triangles, a series of squares, or clouds, footprints, or other shapes either to put wording in, or for decoration. Or, by moving the card over the template and adding further embossing, more complex corners designs can be created.

The finished platemark.

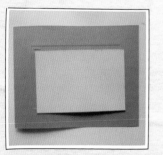

Move the template back from the corner of the platemark and re-emboss around only part of the outline.

Two opposite corners embossed more than once add extra importance to what is enclosed.

Attaching Layers and Using Frames

Instead of writing directly on the card or page, you can write on a chosen paper, and stick that to the surface of the card or page. If you cannot arrange the paper and card so that the grain of each runs in the same direction, attach them with double-sided adhesive tape.

An elegant choice is to leave space between the inner edges of the platemark and the outer edges of paper or layers added inside it {1}. Once the size of the layer that has the writing on it has been established {2}, a piece of thin scrap cardboard is taken and a hole with these same dimensions is cut into it, to make a frame {3}.

This frame is laid over the writing and moved until the balance and margins look correct, and a pencil is then drawn around the inner edge of the frame {4}, so that the written sheet can be trimmed to size {5}.

On many occasions it may be desirable to attach the written sheet to coloured backing before sticking the two into the platemarked area. For the completed card below, an allowance for the extra layer or layers had to be made when determining the finished size of the writing sheet. This example has been written in an Italic style with some Celtic touches (see instructions on pages 64–73).

Card and artwork.

Measure the position of the finished artwork.

Cut a frame the size of the finished artwork.

Mark the boundaries.

Cut the artwork to size.

The completed card.

Double-sided adhesive tape

Because glue may leak through the paper and cause ink, in particular, to run, double-sided adhesive tape is commonly used to attach the writing to the coloured backing stock – but while still aligning the grain of each sheet, if at all possible. Most people find it easiest to trim the coloured layer to size after the writing has been attached, and then fix that inside the sunken platemarked panel with glue, working from the centre outwards, or with tape. This tape is perfect for creating cards that may not be kept forever by the recipient, but for scrapbooks it could lose some or all of its sticking power after a period of time.

Flour paste

Craft bookbinders believe that the most permanent method for adhering paper and card is to mix acid-free PVA with cooked flour paste – up to a 50:50 mixture, until it looks and feels like slime. If you wish to use a similar mixture, or a glue stick to attach a written layer, test a sample before you apply it to the piece you have spent a long time perfecting. The PVA gives the paste extra strength, and the paste gives the PVA a longer setting time and the potential of repositioning.

After attachment by this method, place waxed paper or silicone non-stick baking wrap over the layers and apply pressure while they completely dry – perhaps overnight, under a small pile of heavy books.

 TO MAKE
FLOUR PASTE

YOU WILL NEED:
Plain flour
Double saucepan or steamer

1. Blend 3½oz (100g) plain flour with a little cold water.

2. Make it up to about ⅞ pint (½ litre) with more water and heat it in a double saucepan, or a basin inside a steamer, constantly stirring until it thickens.

3. Remove the paste from the heat and keep it covered while it cools.

4. It will thicken more when it is cold, but can be thinned with water if necessary.

Flour paste can go mouldy rapidly, so it is best to make just enough for two days' use, although it may keep up to a week if sealed in a container and stored in a fridge.

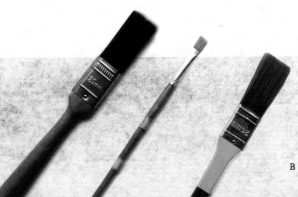

Choosing and Using a Pen

The easiest-to-learn 'thick-and-thin' calligraphy styles are fun to use on cards and scrapbook pages. In this chapter we discuss suitable pen types for the alphabets that follow in Part Two.

All but Copperplate require the use of a pen with an 'edged' nib, which means that it is shaped with a broad, square-cut end like that of a chisel, and constant pressure should be used.

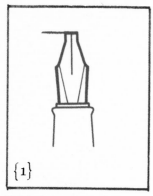

{1}

Hold the pen so that it points parallel to the vertical paper edge and slide it sideways, to produce a thin line.

{2}

Pull the pen down the page to produce an automatic thick line.

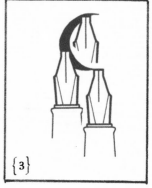

{3}

Point the pen handle down the edge of the paper while drawing half a circle to create a moon shape, widest in the centre and with ends that taper to points.

Note

'Copperplate style' also has lines that are thick and thin, but it is an exception and requires the use of a pointed and flexible nib (right) and a totally different writing technique – pressing harder on the nib to get thick lines and relaxing to get thin ones. The nibs can also be useful for drawing fine shadow lines around letters and stems of decorative trailing plants (see examples on pages 74–9, 133 and 145).

Pen Types: Advantages and Disadvantages

There are many kinds of pen with 'edged' nibs and each has its uses, advantages and disadvantages.

Calligraphy felt pens

These {a} are ideal for an instant letter or word or two: cheap; free-flowing; a range of widths and colours... but they run out and get blunt quickly and never produce letters as crisp as metal nibs.

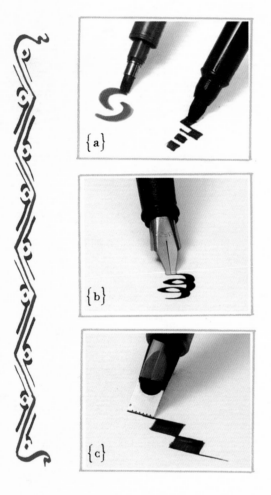

{a}

{b}

{c}

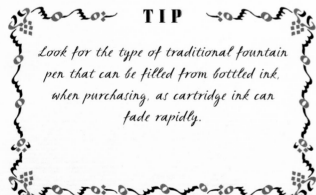

TIP

Look for the type of traditional fountain pen that can be filled from bottled ink, when purchasing, as cartridge ink can fade rapidly.

Note

For the highest quality calligraphy and crispest letter shapes, purists believe that metal dip-nibs give finer thin-letter strokes than fountain pens – but this is rarely a concern for people who wish to add words to cards or scrapbooks.

Calligraphy fountain pens

There are two sorts of fountain pen for calligraphy: the nib of the 'traditional' variety has one or more long slits down the middle {b}, whereas the nib of the 'parallel' pen is made up of parallel plates of metal {c}.

'Traditional' pens are excellent for learning, practice and small- and medium-sized writing but most nibs are for small-sized writing; some inks have a tendency to 'bleed' into papers, producing hairy-looking edges to letter strokes.

Many tutors recommend parallel nibs for beginners: ink flows freely; you can write and shape letters with the corner of the nib; good thin letter strokes, good range of nibs for medium- to larger-sized writing; can be used with gouache paint, watercolour and coloured inks, either by dipping the nib or filling the pen (do not use waterproof inks in fountain pens of any kind); nibs are easily cleaned from one colour to another... but some coloured inks tend to bleed into the paper; the nibs of some other pens are better for really small writing.

Try to avoid letting nibs dry out if there is ink or paint in the pen.

Speedball C0, C1 and C2 dip-nibs

These nibs {a} are quite cheap and come with a built-in reservoir to hold ink or paint; they are sold in most art stores; work well with watercolour, gouache paints and specialist calligraphy ink; have a nice springy feel and are very useful for letters sizes ½–1in (12–25mm) high... but you will need to purchase a separate handle; you cannot write small-sized letters with them; they are a little harder to use than a fountain pen; you learn by experiment how much ink or paint you can put in to achieve consistent letters without blobs; only one or two large letters can be written before you have to re-load them; bleeding may occur with fountain-pen ink (see 'Coping with bleeding' on page 39).

Brause and William Mitchell dip-nibs

Brause nibs {b} are excellent for use with ink or paint; built-in reservoir does not need adjusting; many sizes for small writing – but you will need to purchase a handle and they are harder to use than a fountain pen. With practice William Mitchell Roundhand dip-nibs {c}

produce excellent results with paint and ink and there are a large number of sizes suitable for small writing... but you will need to purchase a separate handle; it is tricky to fit the detachable reservoir; harder to use than a fountain pen; require frequent filling with a brush.

Automatic pens, Coit pens and Speedball Steel Brushes

These {d, e and f} produce excellent results with ink and paint; useful for large sizes of writing for scrapbook headings and special effects... but more expensive than other nibs; may only get one letter per dip or paint loading; it takes practice to use them to produce consistent letter shapes.

Home-made pens

These can be made from balsa wood {g} or bamboo canes {h}. They are cheap; can be cut to special sizes and shapes; work exceptionally well on paper, with ink or paint... but they take some time to make and perfect; wear quicker than metal nibs; you get inky fingers.

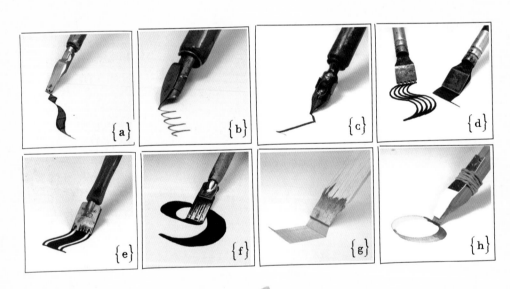

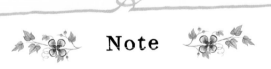

Note

Eventually, you may end up with a collection of most of these pen types. However, if you only ever want to write inside greetings cards and address envelopes in style, you are unlikely to ever use the widest varieties.

TO MAKE
A BALSA-WOOD PEN

 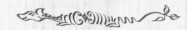

YOU WILL NEED:
A strip of balsa wood
Sharp craft knife, with straight cutting edge

1. Cut a strip of balsa wood in a width that fits your hand and trim the end to your chosen nib width; this strip will probably need to be at least

⅛in (2–3mm) thick. Lay the underside on a hard surface and, using an inflexible, sharp craft knife, or blade with a straight cutting edge, slice the end at an angle of about 30 degrees.

2. Then slice just the tip at a steeper angle of about 60 degrees.

{1}   {2}

The finished pen.

TO MAKE
A BAMBOO PEN

The nibs of pens made from bamboo last longer than
those made from balsa wood before the tip becomes blunt,
particularly if using material purchased from a store,
or which has dried out for several months.

YOU WILL NEED:
A length of dry bamboo garden cane
A sharp craft knife with an inflexible blade
Razor blade
Reservoir cut from a plastic container
Elastic band

1. Cut a length of bamboo about the length of
a normal pen and about ½in (7–12mm) thick,
with a hollow centre.

2. Using a very sharp knife with an inflexible
straight blade, scoop out what will be the
underside of the nib until solid material is
reached. This portion should be completely
flat, to rest on the paper, so remove as little
wood as possible after cutting through the
hollow and any pith that is present.

3. Scrape this surface until it is smooth.

4. Carefully split the end with a razor blade,
probably pulling it about ¼–⅜in (5–8mm).

5. If you like a springy nib and wish to fit a
reservoir, take a sliver off the top, parallel to
the underside of the nib.

6. Rest the underside on a very flat and hard
surface and cut the tip at about 30 degrees,
to make a bevelled, chisel-shaped edge.

7. The final cut is the important one and the
blade must be exceptionally sharp – apply
downward pressure on the blade to remove
the tip of the nib at an angle of about 60 degrees.

8. Trim the sides to width, trying to keep the
split in the nib in the centre.

Fitting a reservoir
To achieve the largest number of letter strokes
written per dip or fill, fit a reservoir in place.
The easiest reservoir to fit is one cut from a
plastic food container with a curved bottom
edge – for example, a yogurt tub.

9. Aim to make the tip of the plastic reservoir
touch the top of the nib a little way along the slit.

10. The reservoir can be held in place with
an elastic band, short length of rubber, or
plastic tube.

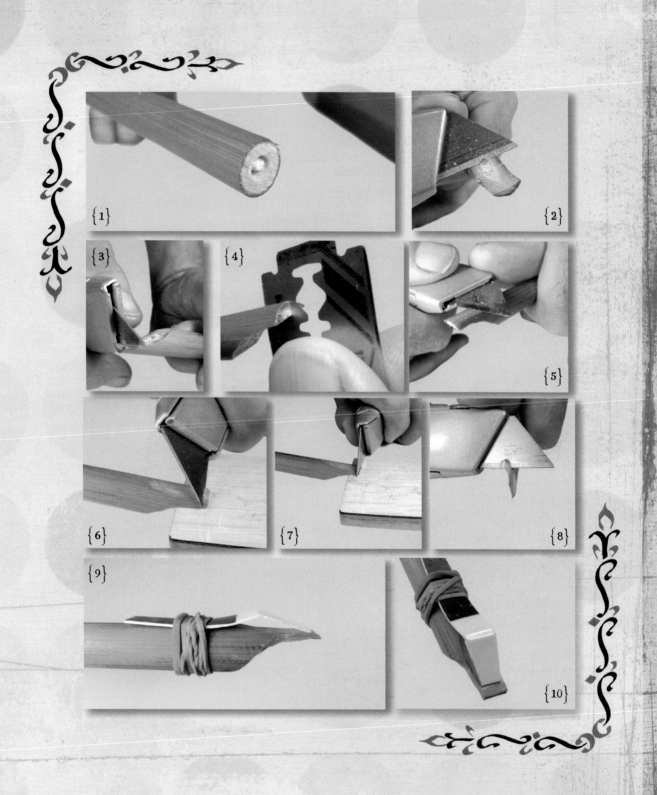

{1}

{2}

{3}

{4}

{5}

{6}

{7}

{8}

{9}

{10}

Using Inks and Coloured Paints

When writing with any of the pens mentioned, aim for a good contrast between the thick and the thin strokes, and sharp ends to letter strokes. These are controlled by the kind of ink or paint that you are writing with, the nature of the paper used and the speed with which you write.

Fountain-pen inks

Each brand of traditional fountain pen is designed to work best with its own brand of fountain-pen ink, but they usually also work well with any fountain-pen ink variety. All these everyday inks are non-waterproof and colours, in particular, are likely to fade. They are sold in bottles and cartridges, and are perfect for practice calligraphy and for greetings cards, envelopes and scrapbook pages that are unlikely to be kept forever.

Each pen manufacturer provides instructions for filling and maintaining their implement, and making it work efficiently. It is always hard, however, to change colours in traditional fountain pens. If the pen has been used for black ink, no matter how many times you wash it out, when you fill with red ink, for example, you will nearly always see a trace of the black in the writing – at least to start with. For this reason, you may eventually purchase a separate pen for each colour you use regularly.

Parallel pens can be dipped into ink or diluted water-based paints without a cartridge in place, or they can be filled according to the manufacturer's directions.

Helping ink to flow

If the ink won't flow smoothly when you use a new fountain pen, or the pen has been left uncapped after use and the ink has dried in the nib and the pen won't restart after refilling, one of these techniques might help:

- Lick and suck the new metal nib for half a minute prior to the first dip, or wipe it with saliva on a tissue (not your finger, which probably has oil from your skin on it).

- Rub the nib with liquid dishwashing detergent, then rinse it off.

- Stand the nib overnight in water with detergent added, and then rinse it. The ink should now flow freely – but might flow too freely for about a page of writing, and produce 'bleeding' (a hairy-looking outline to letters).

- Pass the nib through a match flame for one or two seconds and then quench it in cold water, but note that this method is not suitable for fountain-pen nibs with plastic bodies and can lead to a change in the springiness of the nib.

Note

Never, ever put waterproof ink – including most India ink – in a fountain pen, as a varnish has been added that clogs nibs when it dries. Similarly, acrylic inks will dry to produce a hard-to-remove layer on all equipment used and dip-nibs may need to be washed and cleaned after every line or two of writing to keep them working properly.

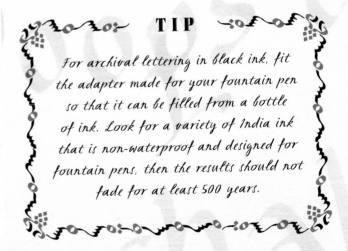

TIP

For archival lettering in black ink, fit the adapter made for your fountain pen so that it can be filled from a bottle of ink. Look for a variety of India ink that is non-waterproof and designed for fountain pens, then the results should not fade for at least 500 years.

Writing in colour with dip-nibs

When writing in colour, and for larger-sized letters, a parallel pen or a dip-nib is generally best. Dip-nibs should not be used with normal fountain-pen ink, as it usually flows out too quickly and produces bleeding and 'thin' letter strokes that are thicker than they should be.

Experiment to find out how much ink manufactured for dip-nibs or paint it is possible to load before it flows out as a blob when you make a mark on paper.

You can dip your nib into a bottle of ink, or you can pour some ink into a bottle cap or shallow container so that it's impossible to dip too far {**a**}. Putting the ink container in a plastic tub, such as the kind used for ice cream, can minimize the risk of damaging splashes and spillages. Or you can fill the nib with the aid of a brush, scraping the bristles against the side of the nib {**b, c** and **d**}. Filling a William Mitchell Roundhand nib is shown in {**e**} and filling an Automatic pen is shown in {**f**}.

Filling dip-nib pens

Writing fluid in a bottle top prevents overloading.

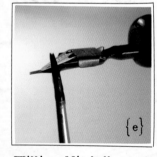
Speedball

Brause

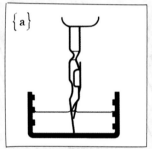
Bamboo

William Mitchell Roundhand nib.

Automatic

Many good varieties of black ink manufactured for calligraphy can be used in dip-nibs, but diluted black gouache is a popular alternative. Most calligraphers add a detachable reservoir to William Mitchell Roundhand nibs to help them hold a reliable volume and to control its flow. Sometimes the reservoirs need to be bent to make them fit properly and stay in the correct place.

The reservoir tip should just touch the underside of the nib without opening the slit, and should be about ⅛in (3mm) from the writing point {**e**}. If it doesn't touch the underside of the nib, the writing fluid will flow too rapidly. Tongue-shaped reservoirs incorporated into a pen handle are even harder to bend to make them fit properly against a nib.

Gouache paint

Many calligraphers use diluted, high-quality gouache paint (professional artist's-quality poster paint) when writing in colour. This is water soluble, made to the highest standards of permanence, available in tubes and is more archival than many coloured inks. A small amount is squeezed on to a lid or palette depression, then water stroked through it with a soft-haired brush until the mixture is just so liquid that it will trickle freely around the edge, or you're sure that if the palette was dropped, the paint would definitely flow on to the floor in an instant. It is impossible to write with paint that is too thick and, as the water blended with the paint evaporates, it may be necessary to add more.

Most colours can be blended by mixing Ultramarine Blue; Prussian Blue; Lemon Yellow; Spectrum Yellow; Flame Red; Alizarin Crimson; Ivory Black; Permanent White. Later you may add others. When buying colours, check the manufacturer's information about the level of permanence, which means how apt they are to fade. Buy the most permanent you can, but if pages or cards are kept in closed albums or boxes, the fading of pigments over time is unlikely to be a problem. Gouache paint can also be diluted to be transparent like watercolours, or you can use artist's quality watercolours, if you wish.

Brown paint purchased in tubes does not usually flow from a nib as well as other colours. Try mixing red, yellow and blue to taste and add just a little brown, such as Vandyke Brown or Havannah Lake and black if you need to.

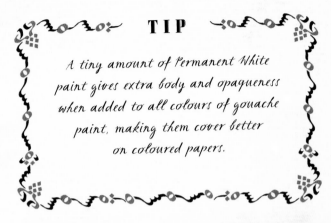

TIP

A tiny amount of Permanent White paint gives extra body and opaqueness when added to all colours of gouache paint, making them cover better on coloured papers.

Blended Prussion Blue and Permanent White gouache paint has been used here, in a mixture of pen types and sizes.

Lemon Yellow blended with Ultramarine Blue gives a good green hue

Spectrum Yellow is brighter and makes the best oranges mixed with Flame Red

Lemon Yellow plus Prussian Blue

Ultramarine Blue mixes with Alizarin Crimson to give a rich purple

Bamboo and balsa-wood pens

These work well on paper and card because they are all of vegetable origin. Stand the pens in the ink or paint for a few minutes before starting to write, so that the liquid soaks into the fibres. Even then, you may only get one letter or a small number of strokes to a dip or fill. It is important to make sure the underside of the nib is really flat and the tip is cut exceptionally cleanly and straight, as described. By cutting notches in the tip of these pens, it is easy to draw decorative letters with hollows in the strokes (see right).

A notch cut in a balsa-wood pen to create hollow letters. This technique was also used to produce the 'A' of 'Angel' on the facing page.

Hollow letters drawn with a notched balsa-wood pen.

TIP

Bamboo pens will stay sharp for quite a long time, but will need the tip re-cut when thin letter strokes look thicker than they should.

Holding a Pen and Sitting to Write

Most people hold a pen with the handle resting between the first two finger joints, on the top knuckle (below left) or in the web of their hand (below right). If you are using a fountain pen, put the cap on the rear end for the best balance. The perfect posture is to have a straight back, with both feet planted flat on the floor. Sloping the writing board makes it easier to see what you are doing and it also helps you to control the flow speed of your writing fluid. You hold your pen more upright when the board is at a shallow angle (below left), so the flow is quicker than if the board is more vertical and the pen handle is closer to the horizontal (below right). The bottom of the board can be rested in your lap, or on the arm of your chair, with the back of the board propped up against a table or a wide shelf. You can then shuffle backwards or forwards to get the optimum board angle. If you are right-handed, it is best if light comes over your left shoulder (but see 'Left-handed Calligraphers' overleaf).

Pen-hold on the knuckle.

Pen-hold in the web of the hand.

Ink can be controlled by board slope: as the board position becomes more upright, the pen is naturally held closer to horizontal, which leads to slower ink flow.

Left-handed Calligraphers

Depending on the letter style and the way a pen is normally held, twisting the paper makes it easier for people who write with their left hand to produce thick and thin lines in the correct places {**a**}.

'Lefties' may also find obliquely cut 'left-handed nibs' can assist in minimizing the need to twist the writing paper to an unfamiliar degree – depending on the way the pen is normally held {**b**}.

Only a few nibs and sizes are made in this way, however, but the writing edge of any home-made bamboo or balsa-wood pen can be cut to whatever angle helps the most to get thick and thin lines in the correct places in letters. Alternatively, some dip-nibs will fit into an angled pen-holder {**c** and **d**}.

The recommended pen-hold for left-handed calligraphers.

Twisting the paper can help left-handed calligraphers draw thin lines at the correct angle.

Oblique fountain-pen nib and a bamboo pen cut for a left-handed calligrapher.

The angled pen-holder helps to line up the nib's slit with the edge of the paper – perfect for Neuland and Uncial styles.

An angled pen-holder used to help draw thin lines at 45 degrees in Italic.

Paper

Cartridge paper is cheap and good to try when practising calligraphy, but experiment with alternatives to find your own favourites for finished work.

For scrapbooking or a special card, archival-quality hot-pressed (smooth-surfaced) 90lb (185gsm) watercolour paper is a favourite of calligraphers, but it is too expensive for practising on. Scrapbook suppliers will offer a range of papers that are of archival quality, but printers may also be able to recommend and sell you varieties that are manufactured to the highest standards. It is advisable to test a single sheet before buying in bulk.

Ingres papers and those designed for artists who use pastels can be good when you want to write on coloured stock. Parchment papers can be suitable for the inside of greetings cards and journaling.

No one paper variety works best for all calligraphers – whether or not a paper suits you can depend on the writing implement you use, the speed you write and the kind of ink or paint you work with.

The paper manufactured for use in photocopiers and laser printers is adequate for pen-play and learning letter shapes, as is layout paper, but you may get some bleeding, especially with fountain-pen ink and large dip-nib and pen sizes.

Coping with 'bleeding'

If bleeding occurs on a paper or card that you want to use for something special, you may be able to solve the problem by sealing the surface of a clean sheet of the material prior to drawing and writing. One way to do this is to spray the stock with artist's 'workable fixative', formulated for preventing charcoal and pastel pictures from smudging. However, a cheaper alternative is to use hairspray. Whichever you choose, it must be left to dry completely before writing.

Avoid using these substances where letters or drawings have been pre-written or decorated with felt or other pens, as the solvent can cause dried inks to run and may also damage photographs, and pencil lines will be hard to erase.

Pastel and watercolour papers usually provide excellent writing surfaces, but handmade papers need to be tested before bulk-buying, as some do not allow clean-edged letters to be drawn.

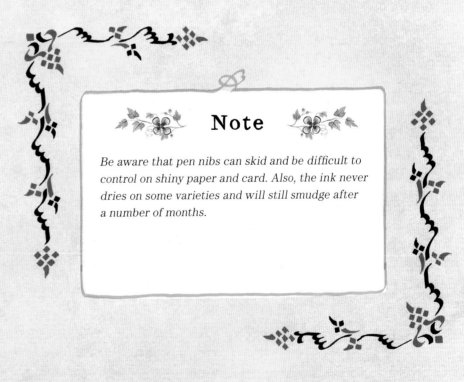

Note

Be aware that pen nibs can skid and be difficult to control on shiny paper and card. Also, the ink never dries on some varieties and will still smudge after a number of months.

Pen Play

After every dip, pen-loading with a brush, or fill from a bottle, you should check that your pen is loaded correctly. To get rid of surplus, aim your pen back at the writing-fluid container and shake the pen with the same action you'd use to throw a dart at a dartboard –

then, on scrap paper, do a little test before writing on the real thing, for example, by drawing a 'V' or zigzag (below left). Stop the test as soon as the corners of the strokes are crisp and the thin lines are thin, or you will run out again.

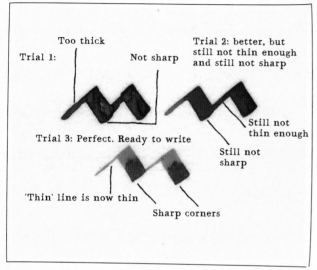

Testing the amount of fluid in a pen (actual size, using a Speedball nib).

TIP

To wipe excess ink or paint from a nib, use something that is not going to shed fibres. A scrap of chamois or other absorbent leather is excellent, and so too is moistened and squeezed-out natural sponge – a make-up sponge, for example.

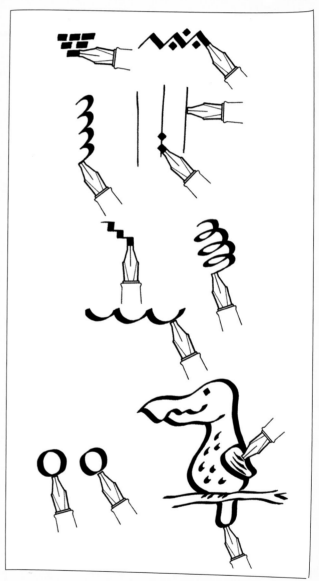

Practice-patterns with an edged pen nib.

Because all calligraphy is drawing letters, it's good to first draw with your pen to get accustomed to using it, prior to learning a writing style with an edged pen nib. Try some patterns, twisting your pen to different angles, to see if you can predict what thickness line it will produce. Keep the handle pointing in one direction as you draw circles and see where the thinnest parts of the letter are created (facing page, right). Sometimes, to produce the thin lines in the place you want them, it's easier to turn the paper than twist your wrist to an unusual position.

If one side of a wide stroke looks uneven, it is probably because that edge of the nib is not in full contact with the paper, so put a little extra pressure on that side of the nib, or reposition the pen in your fingers.

Drawing Guide Lines

Bear in mind that elegant small-sized letters cannot be drawn with a wide, square-cut nib, as the tops of 'e's and 's's, for example, will fill in {a}. And, if you write large-scale letters with a very small nib, they will hardly look thick and thin at all.

For a pleasing look, most alphabets have an ideal letter height compared to the nib width being used. This ratio is called the 'x-height' for each alphabet, measured in nib-widths. This x-height is the height of 'normal-size' small letters, like 'e' and 'x', that fit precisely between top and bottom writing guide lines {b}. You can measure the distance between guide lines in nib-widths, too.

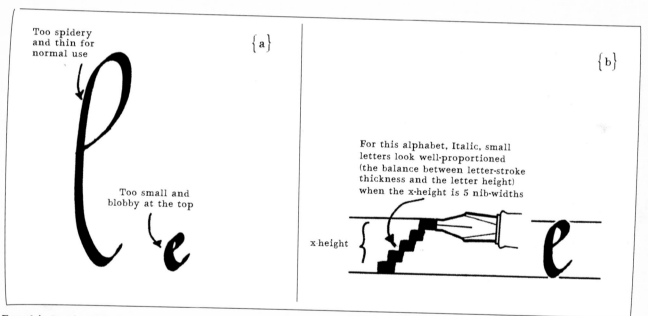

Too spidery and thin for normal use

{a}

Too small and blobby at the top

{b}

For this alphabet, Italic, small letters look well-proportioned (the balance between letter-stroke thickness and the letter height) when the x-height is 5 nib-widths

x-height

For this Italic alphabet, the balance between letter-stroke thickness and the letter height of the small letters looks well-proportioned when the x-height is 5 nib-widths.

Letter-height of all alphabets

The first alphabet for the edged pen is a simplified version of a modern script called Neuland (see pages 48–51), which doesn't have small letters. The height of each letter is 4 nib-widths.

Having filled your chosen pen or nib, you hold it so that the pen's handle points horizontally in the direction the guide lines will be drawn, and then pull it to create the widest block or brick shape that the nib will make, then, for this style, add three more on top so that they just touch each other.

If you draw this stack on a small piece of scrap paper, it can be used as a template to mark out where the writing lines will be dawn. As the alphabet is all capitals, lines of writing can be packed really close together and the style looks best when laid out this way. On the template, a mark also shows the chosen level of the top of the next writing line down the page {a}. This template is then used to mark top and bottom guide-line levels and interline spaces on a strip of scrap paper that is longer than the piece of paper or card that will be written on {b}.

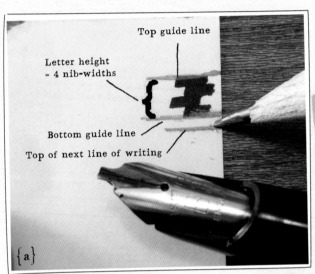

Top guide line

Letter height = 4 nib-widths

Bottom guide line

Top of next line of writing

{a}

Mark the 4 nib-width writing height and line spacing on a scrap-paper template.

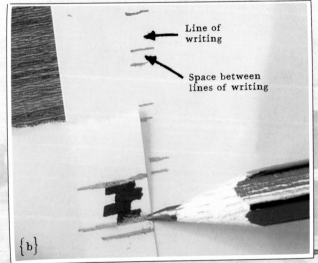

Line of writing

Space between lines of writing

{b}

Transfer measurements to a strip of paper to mark writing-line positions.

The strip and marks are cut in two and taped on both sides of a board, and the writing stock added in between. It is then easy to hold a ruler against the marks and draw the guide lines {a}.

Alternatively, the marks can be held close to the writing sheet and lines marked with the aid of a T-square used against a straight edge of a writing or drawing board {b}.

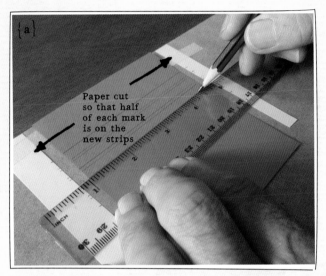

Paper cut so that half of each mark is on the new strips

The marks on the halved strip of paper indicate where to draw the lines on the writing sheet.

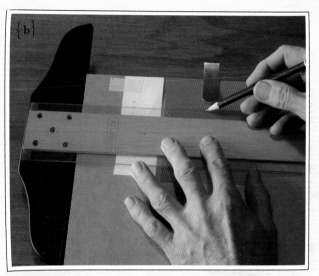

The guide marks are only needed on one side when a T-square is used for drawing the position of writing lines.

TIP

A sharp 4 or 24 pencil is best for lightly ruling lines, as softer pencil leads can smudge, rub into the paper and be hard to erase. Soft white 'stick erasers' are usually excellent for removing pencil lead from between letters, but it is always safest to let ink rest and completely dry and set overnight before using an eraser close to, or over the top of, writing.

Note

Other alphabets may have a different number of nib-widths between guide lines and different line spacing, but their guide lines are constructed in a similar way.

PART TWO

About lettering

The Alphabets

Some letter styles and designs are easier to master than others, but no matter which you use, there are two attributes that make lettering look good: letters in a given style that have a large number of common features and are evenly spaced.

If spacing is even, a wonky letter shape will rarely be noticed. Fortunately, however, it is much easier to achieve pleasing results when writing titles, short verses and labels than it is if you have to write a twelve-verse poem, or to carve letters on a monument with no possibility of another attempt to get it right.

Whether you are an expert calligrapher or just starting, there are times when the brain and hand do not coordinate perfectly. Everyone occasionally produces a misshapen letter – but we aim for perfection.

This does not mean that calligraphy always has to be written painfully slowly, but maybe a little slower than normal handwriting. Remember, each letter is a drawing and it is necessary to take sufficient time to draw it well. The alphabets in this chapter are an excellent introduction to calligraphic penmanship skills and, although no single alphabet is likely to fulfil all purposes, having learnt the formal structure of each first, you can personalize them with added tweaks. Once these alphabets have been learnt, you will be able to copy others that you like in order to develop your toolbox of scripts, ready for selection and use at any time.

Instructions are provided in this chapter for drawing these five useful alphabets.

Neuland is an excellent alphabet for beginner calligraphers because it is easy to get pleasing results. Experts may find it useful, too. The instructions and advice given are also useful when writing in the other styles described in this chapter.

The other alphabets do not have to be learned in the order they are provided, although Celtic uses a similar pen position to that used for Neuland, so is a natural follow-on. Celtic is particularly useful when there is an Irish or Scottish connection, but it is not necessary to confine its use to this kind of subject matter.

Gothic and Italic alphabets require the pen to be held at a different angle to the writing lines. Gothic is decorative and impressive, wonderful for Halloween, old-fashioned style greetings and many heritage locations and occasions, and it has been adopted by teenage culture. It is also good for developing an eye for even letter-spacing.

Italic lettering is rhythmic and easily flourished. It became popular in the twentieth century and is often thought to be the script that can be used for the widest variety of situations and purposes. Copperplate is loopy with oval shapes, constructed totally differently and mostly written as a decorative handwriting style.

Terms Used When Drawing Alphabet Letters

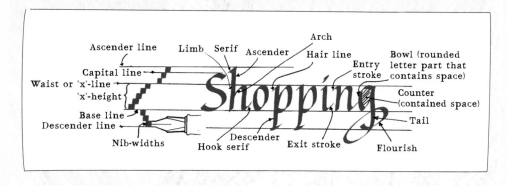

Ascender line · Limb · Serif · Ascender · Arch · Hair line · Bowl (rounded letter part that contains space)

Capital line · Entry stroke

Waist or 'x'-line · 'x'-height

Base line · Counter (contained space)

Descender line · Tail

Nib-widths · Hook serif · Descender · Exit stroke · Flourish

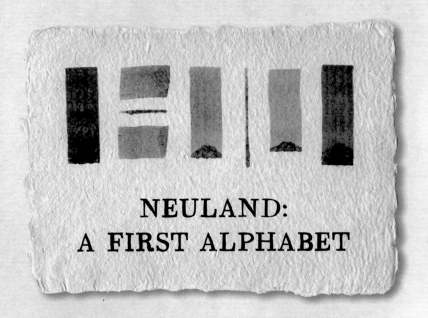

NEULAND: A FIRST ALPHABET

Construction of Letters

In this simple version of Neuland, letters are made up from straight lines and the pen is held so that the thinnest lines the pen can make are parallel to the guide lines. You can see this by looking at the letter 'O' in the alphabet at the top of the facing page.

Although it may seem awkward at first, letter shapes will be perfected most easily if they are initially written with a nib or pen no smaller than ⅛in (3mm) wide – and preferably wider than this. Make each letter a careful and precise drawing.

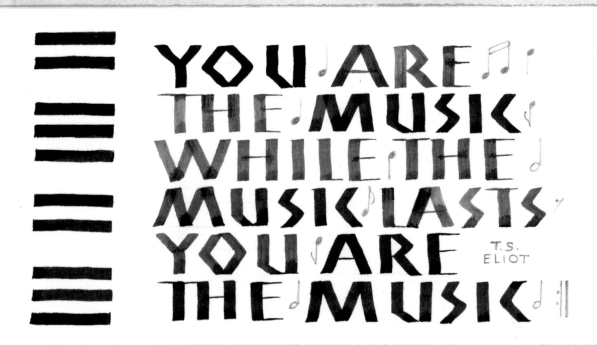

A quotation written in a simple Neuland style. It is best to keep writing lines close together when using this script. Note that the space between the words is smaller than the width of the 'O'.

THE STROKE SEQUENCE FOR NEULAND SCRIPT

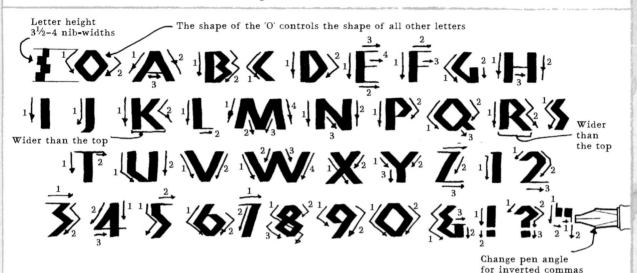

Letter height 3½–4 nib-widths

The shape of the 'O' controls the shape of all other letters

Wider than the top

Wider than the top

Change pen angle for inverted commas

Having found a comfortable place for your writing hand to rest and move the pen, you will write best if it can be kept in that location and the other hand used to reposition the paper after every few letters. To help maintain your hand in the chosen position, as an alternative to completely covering the writing board with a pad of paper, as described in the Tip on page 13, tape a 4in (10cm) square of folded newspaper on this spot and a similar-sized square of cartridge paper over the top.

The handle of the pen should be parallel to the vertical edge of the writing paper for all the letters and numerals.

TIP

Even if a fountain pen or calligraphy felt pen can easily be pushed around on paper, it is good practice to construct letters by only sliding or pulling the pen to make letter strokes. Not only does it help in drawing the letter shape, but also at some time a dip-nib will be used, and it will tend to dig in to the paper surface and create splatters when pushed.

Decorating Neuland

To make this alphabet more decorative you can add
shadow lines (right). If you imagine, for example,
that light is coming from the top left corner of the
page, the shadows will need to be drawn on the
right- and undersides of letters, leaving a little gap.
For beginners, a sharp pencil or coloured pencil is
good for adding these, or a 0.1mm disposable technical-
style pen, gel pen, or similar (but with experience,
you may use a pointed copperplate nib and paint).

Neuland script with shadow lines.

Neuland Variations

ALTERNATIVE SHAPES OF NEULAND LETTERS AND NUMERALS

A A A A A A B C D D E E C
F F G H H H K L L M M
N N N O P Q R S T T U
U V V V W X Y Y Y Y Z
2 3 5 7

Neuland letters can also be made more complex by twisting the pen to create
thick-and-thin strokes in different places and at different angles to those of
the initial, simple version.

May your wishes all
come true
HAPPY
NEW
YEAR
May your wishes all
come true

When writing on projects, alternative versions of letters can be mixed. Here, a mixture of Neuland letter variations have a border in a modernized Celtic 'Uncial' script.

Enlarged versions of the letters can also be drawn and treated decoratively.

CELTIC ALPHABET

Once the simple version of Neuland has been learned, the construction of letters in this modernized version of Celtic 'Half-Uncial' should be straightforward because the pen is held at a similar angle. Although based on the style that monks used around the eighth century in Ireland to produce the *Book of Kells* and in northern England to produce the *Lindisfarne Gospels*, it can still look modern.

As when writing Neuland, the pen is normally held with a pen angle of 0 degrees, so its handle is at right angles to the guide lines, and the thinnest lines the nib makes run along the guide lines. Some calligraphers, make these thin lines slope the tiniest amount, but not more than 10 degrees.

FIRST STEPS IN LEARNING CELTIC CALLIGRAPHY STYLE

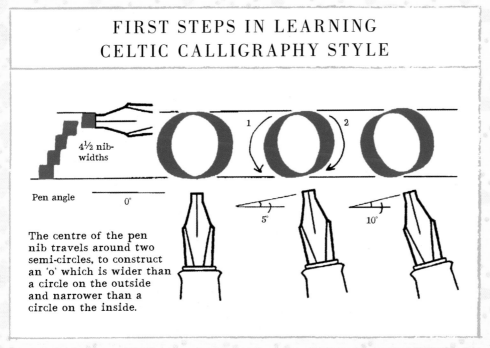

4½ nib-widths

Pen angle ———— 0°

The centre of the pen nib travels around two semi-circles, to construct an 'o' which is wider than a circle on the outside and narrower than a circle on the inside.

5° 10°

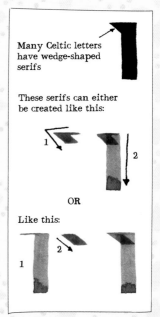

Many Celtic letters have wedge-shaped serifs

These serifs can either be created like this:

1 2

OR

Like this:

1 2

The wedge-shaped serifs are a special feature of Celtic calligraphy.

Whichever pen-angle is chosen for the 'o' must be maintained for the rest of the alphabet.

CONSTRUCTION OF CELTIC SMALL LETTERS

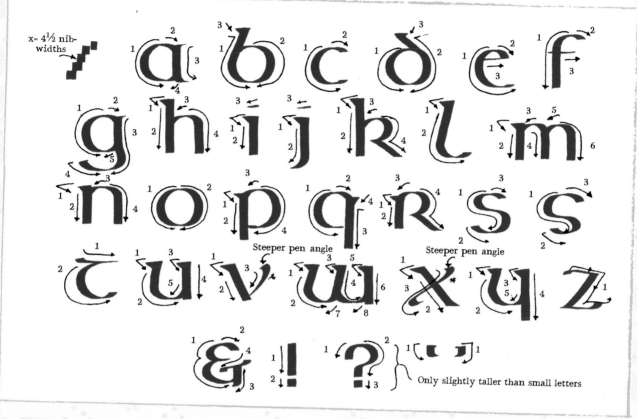

x= 4½ nib-widths

Steeper pen angle

Steeper pen angle

Only slightly taller than small letters

You don't always have to write to a fixed size, or on straight lines. This is background journaling for a scrapbook page.

An example of Celtic script on a card.

CONSTRUCTION OF CELTIC CAPITAL LETTERS

6 nib-widths

A B C D E F
G H I J K L M
N O P Q R S
T U V W X Y
Z 1 2 3 4 5
6 7 8 9 0

Numerals
can be all the
same height,
if preferred.

Capitals are only 1–1½ nib-widths taller than small letters.

SPECIAL NOTES

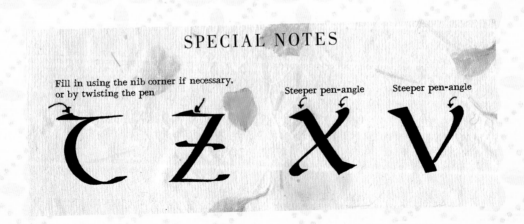

Fill in using the nib corner if necessary,
or by twisting the pen

Steeper pen-angle

Steeper pen-angle

T Z X V

Many of the capitals are large versions of the small letters. It may be necessary to twist your nib to make serifs on the top of 'T', 'Z' and maybe 'D' (or draw from the wet ink with the corner of the nib) and also to construct some sloping strokes on letters. Adding colour in or around letters is optional (below).

A large number of letters can be treated this way, or just an occasional one or two in a longer piece of writing to give a feeling that jewels have been scattered on the page – and of course, colours chosen can be subtle variations of a single hue, or contrasting and brilliant.

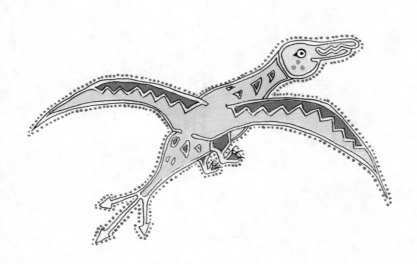

Wishing you a long, happy and healthy Retirement

Colouring inside small or capital letters can be an attractive addition.

Celtic Variations

ABCDEFGHIJKLMN
OPQRSSTTUVWXYZ

A variation of the Celtic script, drawn with a disposable fibre-tip pen that gives a constant line thickness.

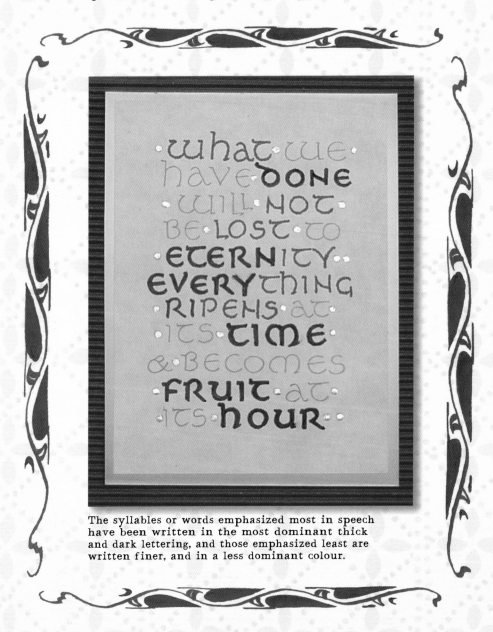

The syllables or words emphasized most in speech have been written in the most dominant thick and dark lettering, and those emphasized least are written finer, and in a less dominant colour.

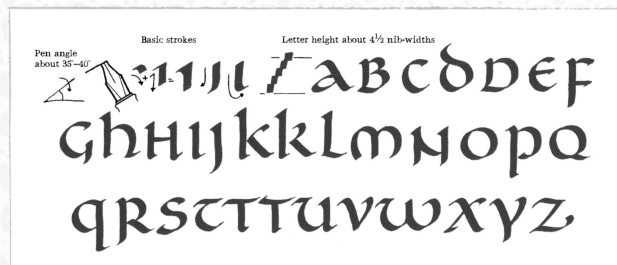

Pen angle about 35°–40°

Basic strokes

Letter height about 4½ nib-widths

A variation drawn with a sloping pen angle and rounded serif shapes.

Pen angle about 35°–40°

Basic strokes

Letter height about 6 nib-widths

A variation with triangular serifs on the bottom of some strokes, as well as the top.

GOTHIC ALPHABET

This angular and decorative style is also called 'Black Letter'. Some people also call it 'Old English' – but they shouldn't, because that's the name of a typeface with capitals that you can't copy with a straight-cut calligraphy pen nib. Gothic may be hard to read when a text is long, but it is very useful for headings, titles and cards (see scrap pages on pages 63 and 91 and cards on pages 111 and 127). Many versions of the Gothic script can be found in books on calligraphy and, after trying this one, copying any other one that is seen, or using its features to produce your own, should be easy.

FIRST STEPS IN LEARNING GOTHIC CALLIGRAPHY STYLE

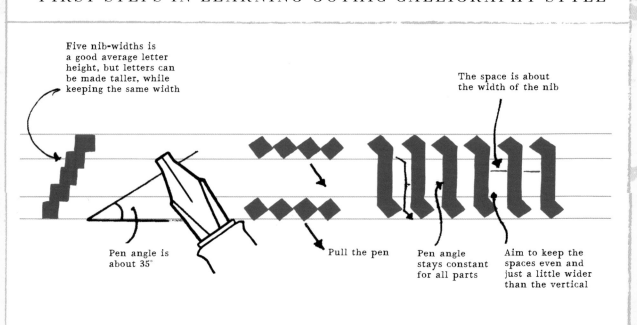

Five nib-widths is a good average letter height, but letters can be made taller, while keeping the same width

The space is about the width of the nib

Pen angle is about 35°

Pull the pen

Pen angle stays constant for all parts

Aim to keep the spaces even and just a little wider than the vertical

The x-height of letters can be varied according to personal preference, but 5 nib-widths is a good height to start with. For this version, the pen angle is maintained at about 35 degrees, as shown on the facing page. Hold the pen nib stationary for a fraction of a second, or remove it, at each direction change.

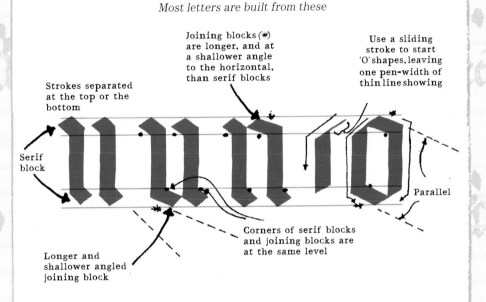

THE CONSTRUCTION OF GOTHIC LETTER PARTS

Most letters are built from these

Joining blocks (✳) are longer, and at a shallower angle to the horizontal, than serif blocks

Use a sliding stroke to start 'O' shapes, leaving one pen-width of thin line showing

Strokes separated at the top or the bottom

Serif block

Parallel

Longer and shallower angled joining block

Corners of serif blocks and joining blocks are at the same level

A Gothic alphabet has been used on this greetings card.

CONSTRUCTION OF GOTHIC SMALL LETTERS

Flattened tops – almost horizontal

SPECIAL NOTES

Steeper than a serif block

Should be equal

Guide line runs along the top of the bar

e g t

CONSTRUCTION OF GOTHIC CAPITAL LETTERS

Capitals are only 1–1½ nib widths taller than small letters.

SPECIAL NOTES

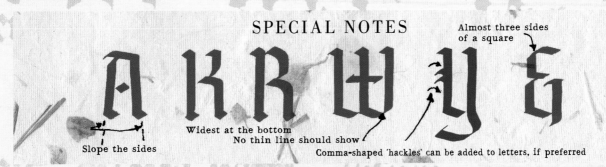

Almost three sides of a square

Slope the sides

Widest at the bottom

No thin line should show

Comma-shaped 'hackles' can be added to letters, if preferred

MODERNIZED NUMERALS TO ACCOMPANY GOTHIC

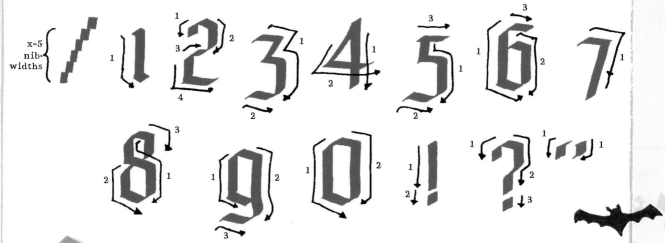

Some numbers look best when they are level (2661), while others look more interesting on two levels (2365).

Decorate and embellish your letters for fun.

Curves added to 'h', 'm', 'n', 'v' and 'w' can help legibility, but decorations can be added for fun.

Ape Bee Crane Deer Eel Frog Guppy Hake Ibis Jabiru Koala Llama Moth Newt Otter Pelican Quoll Robin Salmon Tench Unicorn Viper Walrus X-ray Yabby Zebra

Reduced serifs aid even spacing

Celtic style capitals can also be used with Gothic calligraphy.
Note that the spacing between words is about the size of a small letter 'o'.

All the gouache colours used to write on this scrapbook page had
Permanent White added to them to aid covering.

ITALIC ALPHABET

Although Italic calligraphy can be turned into Italic handwriting, the letters of the two are constructed slightly differently. Originally, Italic was only a hand-writing style in use in the mid- to late 1500s, and it was written very, very small in size with a blunt quill cut from a swan or goose feather, so the pen could be pushed around the curved parts of letters. This is much harder to do successfully when writing larger letters with modern metal nibs, so again, it's good to pull all strokes (though most calligraphers do take the risk and push a pen for some strokes from time to time).

Drawing the majority of Italic calligraphy letter strokes separately also means that elegant starting and finishing serif stokes can be added to letters, which would not be possible if letters were run from one to another in handwriting.

The special features of Italic calligraphy are that 'o' is elliptical and the right side of 'n' bounces and branches right from the bottom of the first vertical. The pen-angle is maintained at 45 degrees and 5 nib-widths is a good x-height (see alphabet on facing page).

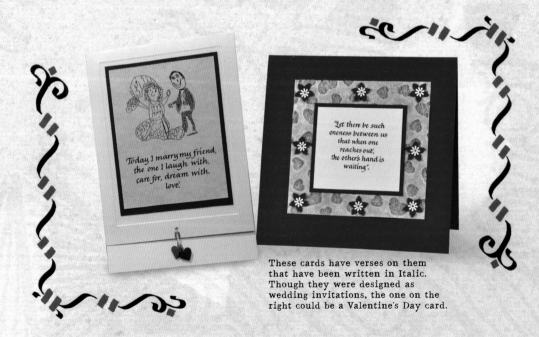

These cards have verses on them that have been written in Italic. Though they were designed as wedding invitations, the one on the right could be a Valentine's Day card.

THE PRINCIPLES OF ITALIC LETTER CONSTRUCTION

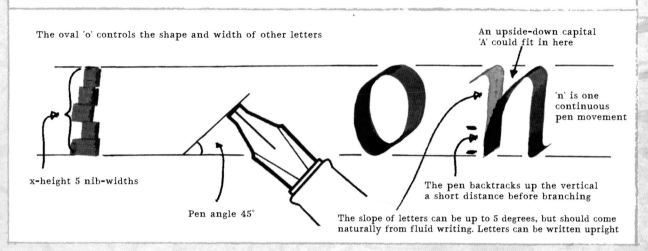

The oval 'o' controls the shape and width of other letters

An upside-down capital 'A' could fit in here

'n' is one continuous pen movement

x-height 5 nib-widths

Pen angle 45°

The pen backtracks up the vertical a short distance before branching

The slope of letters can be up to 5 degrees, but should come naturally from fluid writing. Letters can be written upright

CONSTRUCTION OF ITALIC SMALL LETTERS

✳ Only 'n', 'm', 'r' and 'x' have a rounded entry

SPECIAL NOTES

Top of the bar touches the writing line

Slopes downhill

Top and bottom are parallel

Taller, with a simpler tail

The starting stroke of the bowl of 'p' begins at the bottom guide line and travels up the vertical, and branches like 'n'

Smaller area than the bottom

Balanced with the top

Hits bottom guide line here

Straight but downhill at start

Branch at same height, higher than 'n'

The crossing is above halfway

Zero is more circular than 'o'

CONSTRUCTION OF ITALIC CAPITAL LETTERS

a A B C D E F
G H I J K L M
N O P Q R S T
U V W X Y Z &

Capitals are only 1–1½ nib-widths taller than small letters

Italic capitals are about 6½ pen widths high and, like most capitals, they are best drawn only 1–1½ nib-widths taller than the small letters. They have similar proportions to classic Roman capitals, but all have been compressed a little from side to side to match the elliptical nature of 'O', and sloped just a fraction (but not as much as the small letters).

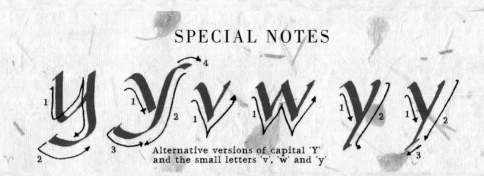

Alternative versions of capital 'Y'
and the small letters 'v', 'w' and 'y'

talking time

time

Italic calligraphy drawn as separate letters with serifs can be made to flow like handwriting by elongating exit strokes, then dropping the next letter on the end – if it misses, it doesn't matter because the most important thing is to make the spacing look even.

Avoid joins at the top guide line, as shown here: it looks more casual than other letter combinations and it is hard to make spacing look even this way.

Note

You don't always have to use pens. This Italic-style 'R' was written using two pencils taped together but held like a pen. The patterns were then added with black fine-writers and the guide lines erased. The original was 3 x 3in (7.5 x 7.5cm).

Italic has only
been a popular calligraphy
style since the mid-1900s, and people
are still finding ways to add their personal
touches. By minimizing the hooked terminal
strokes or replacing them with more complex
serifs, Italic letters look more formal.

SOME ITALIC ASCENDER AND DESCENDER VARIATIONS

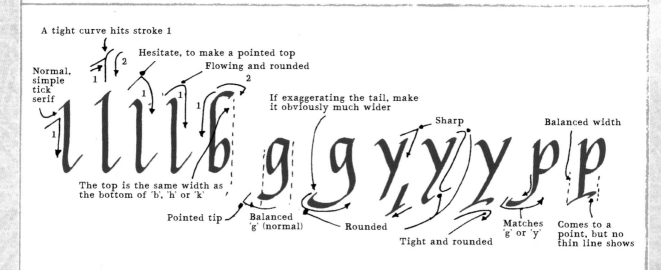

A tight curve hits stroke 1

Hesitate, to make a pointed top

Flowing and rounded

Normal,
simple
tick
serif

If exaggerating the tail, make
it obviously much wider

Sharp

Balanced width

The top is the same width as
the bottom of 'b', 'h' or 'k'

Pointed tip

Balanced
'g' (normal)

Rounded

Tight and rounded

Matches
'g' or 'y'

Comes to a
point, but no
thin line shows

ABCDEFGHHIJKLM
NOPQRSTUVWXYZ
abcdefghijklmno
pqrrstuvwxyyz

This version of Italic has Celtic touches added to some letters, which can be written carefully, or more flamboyantly when confidence has been gained.

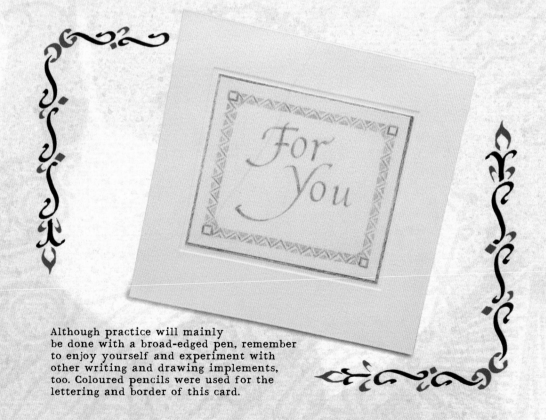

Although practice will mainly be done with a broad-edged pen, remember to enjoy yourself and experiment with other writing and drawing implements, too. Coloured pencils were used for the lettering and border of this card.

Flourishes

Each calligrapher has favourite flourishes for use with Italic calligraphy, but they cannot be added to all letters: just because letters like 'y' can easily have the tails flourished and looped, it doesn't mean that it should be done on every letter in a title or piece of writing. Though well-practised calligraphers can draw very complicated flourishes, they chiefly use simple ones.

Start with a small curve about ⅙ of a circle

Hesitate before adding the downstroke 'comma'

Long stretched 's' shapes

Add flags

The 's' shape cuts off any protruding thin lines

Add extras

These flourishes look best when as wide as the letter and very tall – 5 times the 'x' height, perhaps

The secret to elegant flourishes is to imagine that you are creating part of a pattern like a figure 8, or a spiral that could be continued after the pen is removed from the paper. It helps if you actually do continue tracing the pattern in mid-air, as the pen is lifted at the completion of the drawing.

'Flags' can be added to the top of letters, if it is appropriate (as well as any of a large range of alternatives that start as a long skinny 'S').

It is much easier to keep letters looking elegant if, when two letters together could both be flourished, only the first one is decorative.

1. Omit ascender to be flourished

2. Turn the work upside down

Complete the letter

3. The completed word

Hayden

A significant gap

All spaces are about the same size ✓

Too close and 'blobby' ✗

To add big loops to the tops of letters, an easy option is to turn the work upside down and then add the extra stroke parts in the same way that the tail of a letter is flourished.

Try to make bold crossovers without creating tiny areas of enclosed space.

To fill a space, a flourish can be aimed at a letter without touching it (left), but it is necessary to make sure that in doing so, an 'a' is not made to look like a 'g', or a 'd', for example. If you see a flourish pattern that you'd like to do yourself, steadily trace it about ten times and then do one freehand – repeat this three or four times, and it should come naturally.

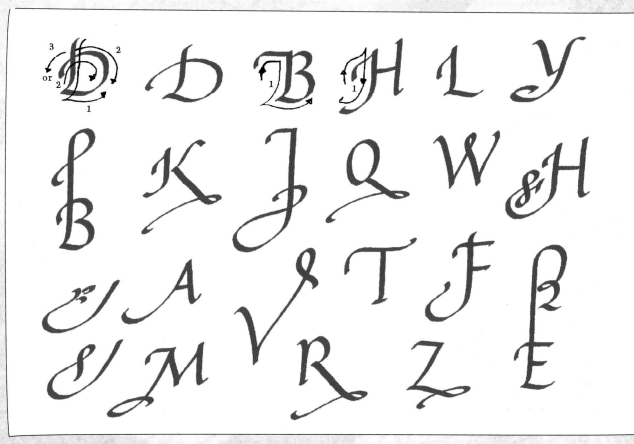

Flourishes for Italic capitals – some can be used on a number of letters. The pen may catch in the paper fibres, but you can try pushing some of these extended letter and flourish strokes, if you wish.

The two alphabets on this page provide a good contrast and accompaniment to Italic, when writing in 'all capitals' is needed. The diamond-shaped blocks do not have to be added to the top one.

RUNNING BOOK HAND 1

ABCDEFGHIJ KLMNOPQR STUVWXYZ

It is helpful to collect pictures of variations that you admire, and ways that they can be used. The diamond additions used here and on the card below can be useful, but pen-angle changes are needed to add them to some letters. This alphabet has been written a fraction under 4 nib-widths high.

JUST TO SAY ...

RUNNING BOOK HAND 2

ABCDEFGHIJ KLMNOPQRS TUVWXYZ

This alphabet is also written a little less than 4 nib-widths high. It has larger serif feet, more rounded corners and some letters are a different shape from the alphabet above. The envelopes on the facing page use this alphabet.

73 Marine Drive
Off Old Bay Road
Linford
Near Watamoke
7329

NEW ZEALAND

MR &
MRS JOE & MARY WISTON

136 Lake View Crescent · Willowbrook · WA 6998

AUSTRALIA

When writing in all capitals it is often most effective when the writing lines are close together (left) – they can even touch each other.

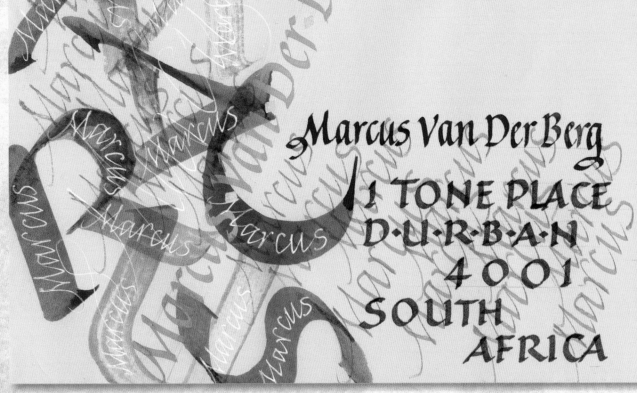

Marcus Van Der Berg

1 TONE PLACE

D·U·R·B·A·N

4 0 0 1

SOUTH

AFRICA

The large jumbled letters on the left are written with a balsa-wood pen dipped in diluted Prussian Blue gouache. The smaller blue writing was added with a William Mitchell dip-nib, the black with a fountain pen, the white with a gel pen and the repeating casually and rhythmically written versions of 'Marcus' in the background with a worn-out calligraphy felt-pen.

COPPERPLATE ALPHABET

To avoid mixing styles, it is best to wait until you are totally familiar with other alphabets before attempting this alphabet. In particular, if you are used to writing Italic, there is potential to make Copperplate ovals and exit strokes look too pointed.

Conversely, those who write Copperplate prior to learning Italic, can make their Italic too rounded. With that proviso, the following instructions will enable you to make a start and produce some impressive cards and pages.

Examples of Copperplate calligraphy by Douglas Eising. The hand-marbled paper used on the front of the card adds a decorative effect.

Pens and ink

Copperplate was first developed in the mid-1500s by printers who engraved the letters into sheets of copper to print from, and added lots of bonus loops and decorative twirls. New pens had to be designed to write in a similar fashion. There are now brands of fountain pen, with very pointed and flexible nibs, that can be used to write Copperplate. However, whether or not you find them satisfactory will depend on the way you hold your pen and whether you can aim the slit in the nib along the slope lines. Only a specialist pen shop will be able to advise what would be good to use, and you need to test a few combinations of dip-nib and ink varieties, to see which work best for you before purchasing.

'Elbow' Copperplate nibs and angled pen-holders (top right) can help right-handed calligraphers to align a dip-nib more easily, and these generally produce more contrast between thick and thin letter elements than fountain pens do.

'Gillott 404' nibs are popular for large-sized writing and 'Hunt Imperial 101' for smaller letter heights, but try as many different flexible and pointed nibs as you can until you find your own favourites.

Ink needs to be thicker than for other styles and brushed onto the underside. You can let some evaporate, or mix black or another colour of gouache paint with water to a consistency that flows as you like it. Iron Gall ink is a favourite of many who enjoy this writing style, but standard ink varieties made by a range of manufacturers work well, too.

Elbow Copperplate nib   **Angled pen-holder**

Fitting a reservoir

This is not essential, but you can add a William Mitchell reservoir to your nib to hold more ink and control the flow. However, as they are not made to fit these nibs, you'll need to bend the reservoir out of shape and fiddle with it until it looks as shown below, with the tongue just touching the inside of the nib.

A **William Mitchell** reservoir, bent to fit an elbow nib. It must hold firm centrally and touch the slit without opening the two nib halves.

Note

Copperplate is based on an oval-shaped 'O' on a big 55 degree slope (or 35 degree off the vertical), which some people find very hard to maintain on all letters. It will help if you give yourself as many slope guide lines as you need, or construct a guide line sheet and put it under your work.

You will find that all small letters are made up of one or more of the strokes shown below, so it is a good idea to practise them carefully before writing letters. Do not be afraid to trace over these letters a few times, before writing one freehand, then trace several more times and do one freehand. This will help lock the shape in your brain and you soon won't need to trace.

FIRST STEPS IN LEARNING COPPERPLATE

Letter slope and pen held at 55°

Entry stroke

Build pressure

Release pressure

As thin as pen can make

Start here

Fill with extra pressure

Build pressure gradually

Release pressure gradually

Start as a small spiral with pressure

Tight spiral with extra pressure

COPPERPLATE LOWER-CASE ALPHABET

a b c d e f g h i j k

l m n o p q r s t u

v w x y z ! ? ‚‚

Many small letters are written in a single stroke, but the Special Notes on the facing page should be read before attempting to construct any of them.

76

COPPERPLATE UPPER-CASE ALPHABET

You will find many varieties of capitals, but their shapes and loops are always built from ellipses. Numerals are halfway between capitals and small letters in size.

SPECIAL NOTES FOR LOWER-CASE LETTERS

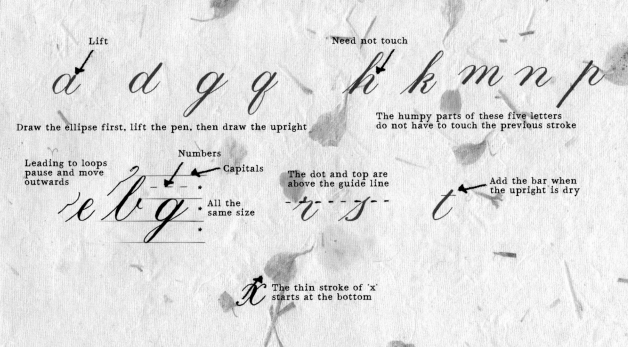

Lift

Need not touch

Draw the ellipse first, lift the pen, then draw the upright

The humpy parts of these five letters do not have to touch the previous stroke

Leading to loops pause and move outwards

Numbers

Capitals

All the same size

The dot and top are above the guide line

Add the bar when the upright is dry

The thin stroke of 'x' starts at the bottom

Spacing of words and letters

Keep the spaces between letters and words small
(you don't need to join all letters in words and can
break wherever you need to) but spaces between
lines should be on the large side. Numerals are
halfway between capitals and small letters in height.
You will find many variations of capitals, but they
are always built from ellipses.

And let there be no purpose in friendship save the deepening of the spirit.

Practise by writing just two or three short words
together to start with, before writing longer sayings
and texts.

Hand-drawn calligraphy always looks impressive on greeting
cards or journaling on a scrapbook page, and a beautifully
written envelope will make the recipient feel special.

It is better to light a candle than to complain about the darkness

This card was written by Douglas Eising, who
is left-handed. Copperplate is often easier for
left-handed people than some other styles.

Mr. and Mrs. William Reese
627 Kewanna Drive
Jeffersonville, Indiana 47130

Jan Hurst wrote this envelope. All calligraphers
give their alphabets personal touches, especially
Copperplate capitals.

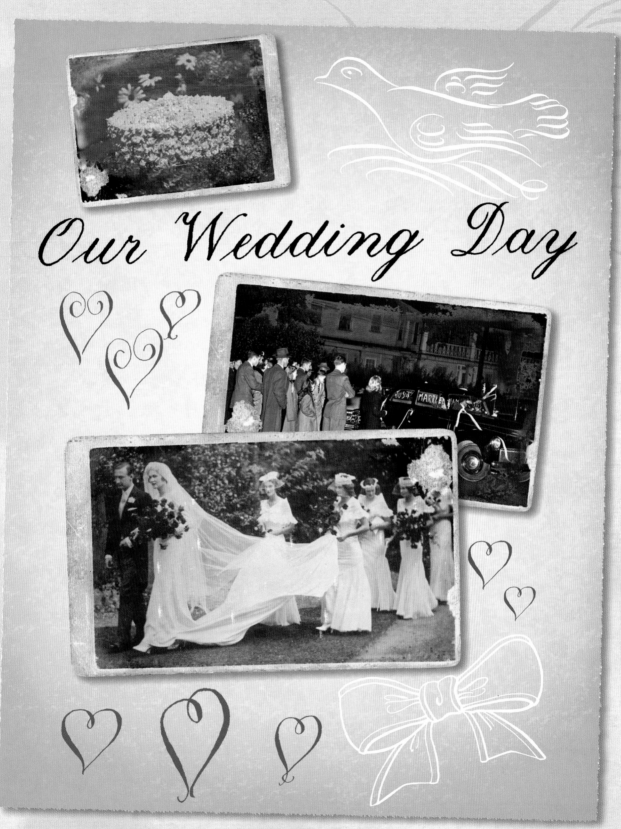

Our Wedding Day

This scrapbook page could be part of a spread featuring journaling. When drawing with a Copperplate nib it may be necessary to turn the paper upside down, or at different angles, to get the thick and thin parts of lines where you want them to be.

Using Your Calligraphy

Whatever style of lettering is being used, ultimately the creation of even spaces while drawing one letter after another has to be done 'by eye', but this chapter includes a few tricks of the trade that can help.

Spacing Letters and Words

Incorrectly spaced letters in words always stand out. It doesn't matter too much if one or two letters are imperfectly shaped, or there are inconsistencies in height. If the spacing between letters looks even and all letters are on a constant slope the whole effect will be impressive and pleasing to the eye. It is the even spacing that makes medieval manuscripts like the one below, look fantastic.

Part of a medieval manuscript written in about AD 1280 (actual size).

Traditional spacing

What your brain tells you is the edge of a letter, is often not the true edge. For example, if you use vertical dashed lines to mark the apparent width of a capital 'A', the edges are positioned halfway down each sloping side. It is the same for other letters, as shown below.

This shows the optical edge of letters with sloping strokes. The dashed lines must cross the sloping lines of the letters at their mid-point, on the outside edge of the letter.

Because of the curved nature of a circular 'O', the width of this letter appears narrower than the extreme edges, too. If you put an 'O' into a square, as shown below, the top shaded section outside the circle has the same area as the shaded section inside the circle and these cancel each other out. This means that the perceived edge of the letter is where the black dashed lines are drawn, and the visual width of the letter is the distance between the two dashed lines. Other curved letters also have perceived edges that are not at the limit of each bulge (bottom left), and when letters have open ends, your eye tells you that the vertical marking the letter's extremity should be drawn inside the actual measurable width (bottom right).

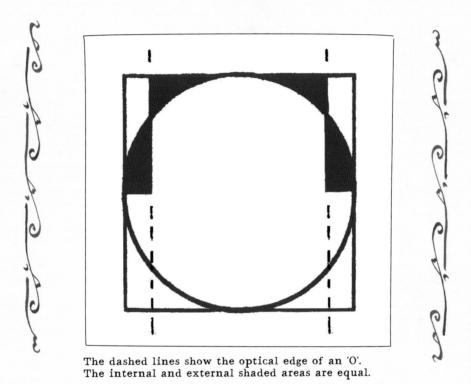

The dashed lines show the optical edge of an 'O'.
The internal and external shaded areas are equal.

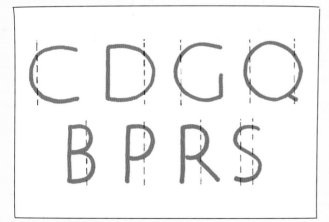

The optical edges of the curved portions of letters.

The optical edges of cutouts, or open sections of letters.

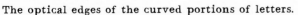

The same applies to small letters, shown in Italic style (below), where the aim has been to make all gaps between the perceived letter edges look the same, without measuring them. Eventually, with careful practice, perfect positioning of the start of each letter will become instinctive. Unfortunately this skill takes time to cultivate, and only after a work has been completed do you find out if errors of judgment have been made. It is impossible to develop complete machine accuracy, no matter how many years calligraphy is practised.

The optical edges of small letters.

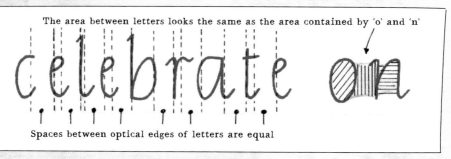

The area between letters looks the same as the area contained by 'o' and 'n'

Spaces between optical edges of letters are equal

Imagining the optic edges of letters will help you to achieve even spacing.

Now that you've passed your Driving Test...

celebrate!

Carefully!

Evenly spaced Italic has been used for this card.

Note

Your judgment is bound to be imperfect from time to time, but don't get disheartened – if you can see where your work can be improved, and try not to make the same mistake again, you will get better.

On some occasions you may want to draw all letters between straight guide lines, to produce perfect horizontal stripes of words, but that is not always necessary.

There are alternatives and you are supposed to have fun, so experiment. Still try to make spaces look even between letters, but don't worry about their height or level (below).

MAY C·A·L·M BE SPREAD AROUND YOU MAY THE SEA GLISTEN LIKE GREENSTONE AND THE SHIMMER ᵒf SUMMER DANCE ACROSS YOUR PATH

This creative lettering concentrates on letter shape and even spacing, rather than consistent letter height.

Quick Fixes

Uneven spacing

The good news for card-makers and scrapbookers is that, if lettering is not evenly spaced, it is often fixable without re-writing. This technique might not be appropriate for a heading on a government charter, but here's a top tip: for a card or scrapbook page title, you can add colour, as shown on page 55, for use with Celtic calligraphy.

All these particular spaces look larger than other spaces

Space is too small

This title has flawed letter spacing.

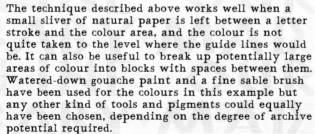

Adding darker colour in the excessive gaps, pale colour – or no colour at all – in the 'too small' gaps, and something in between in the normal spaces this can be corrected and the words appear to be perfectly spaced.

The technique described above works well when a small sliver of natural paper is left between a letter stroke and the colour area, and the colour is not quite taken to the level where the guide lines would be. It can also be useful to break up potentially large areas of colour into blocks with spaces between them. Watered-down gouache paint and a fine sable brush have been used for the colours in this example but any other kind of tools and pigments could equally have been chosen, depending on the degree of archive potential required.

Another way to fix spaces that look too large is to add an appropriate decoration or embellishment. Here, the gap between the 'M' and the 'O' is too big and the first half of the 'M' is a bit too wide.

The wording has been trimmed and applied to a card, and spacing optically corrected with embellishments. A heart entering the space below left of the 'M' helps make the interior area look the same as that in the second half.

Extra-wide spacing

If just a short word or two needs to be added to a card
or scrapbook page, an easy way of creating evenly spaced
letters is to leave much bigger gaps between them than
usual – perhaps about three times the normal amount,
although other widths can be tried, too. Whatever size
space is chosen, mark this width on a small piece of paper.
After the first letter has been written, hold the left-hand
mark in line with the letter's right-hand optical edge and
the other mark will tell you where the optical edge of the
next letter should be when you draw it (right and below).

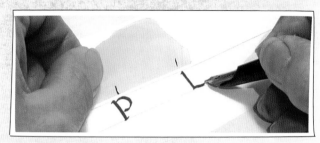

Creating even spaces between widely separated letters.

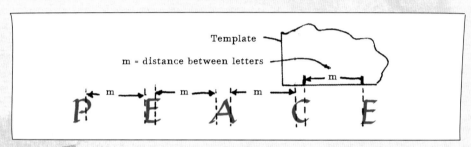

Template

m = distance between letters

The finished word.

The technique described above has been used here, resulting
in well-spaced letters in a pleasing arrangement.

HALLOWEEN

Here, the word 'Halloween' is well spaced. It looks particularly even because
the space between letters is the same as the optical width of the 'O'.

HALLOWEEN

For some purposes, it may be desirable to reduce the spaces to shorten the length
of a word, but then the 'L's might collide. To prevent that problem, their bases
can be made narrower or staggered, as shown here, but if the space between letters
is reduced too much, the space inside the 'O' could stand out as being extra large.

Overlapping letters

If left in their traditional proportions, some letter combinations like 'LA', 'TT', 'TV' and 'LT' can control the spacing of all other letters on the page and perhaps make the text take up more space than desired.

To remedy this, the bottoms of 'L's and the tops of 'T's can be shortened or staggered, letters can be overlapped, 'A's and 'V's can be narrowed and others shortened and tucked under each other, as shown below.

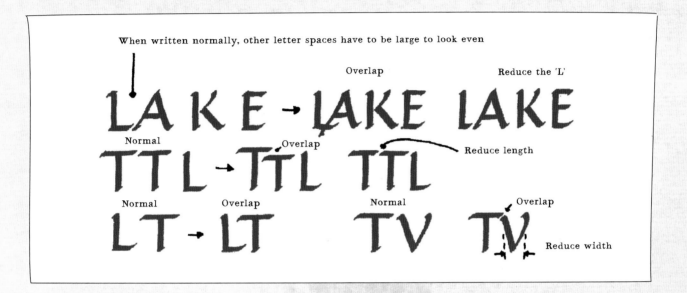

When written normally, other letter spaces have to be large to look even

Overlap

Reduce the 'L'

LA K E → LAKE LAKE

Normal   Overlap   Reduce length

TTL → TTL TTL

Normal   Overlap   Normal   Overlap

LT → LT   TV   TV   Reduce width

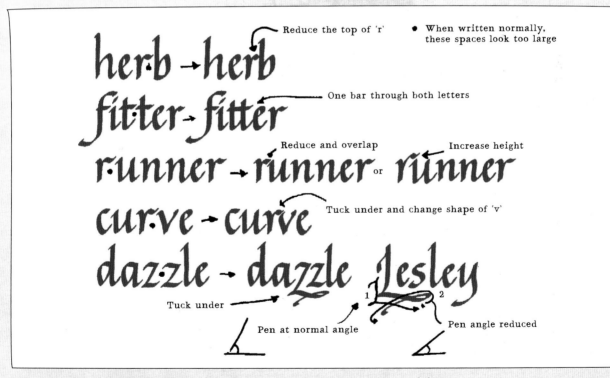

Reduce the top of 'r'

When written normally, these spaces look too large

herb → herb

One bar through both letters

fitter → fitter

Reduce and overlap   Increase height

runner → runner or runner

Tuck under and change shape of 'v'

curve → curve

dazzle → dazzle Lesley

Tuck under

Pen at normal angle   Pen angle reduced

These techniques for creating even letter spacing can be used when writing in any style. Overlapping also helps to save space when writing in capitals and small letters (see 'Lesley', bottom right). Changing the proportions and shapes of some small letters (as in the bottom line) and making joins, are other ways to make spacing look even.

Using a Light-box to Help with Spacing

To use this method, first carefully write the chosen word or words on scrap paper (with guide lines if desired) and then check the result to see if there are any letters or spaces that need adjusting. Some gaps between letters may look too large or too small (as in Version 1 below), or perhaps a letter is misshapen. If the latter is the case, write the letter again somewhere on the scrap paper until the version is satisfactory and you have decided which spacing to adjust when the words are traced. Then, trace the first letter, using tracing paper

and black or dark-coloured ink. Again, check the gap between this and the following letter. If the letter shape and the gap are perfect, trace the next letter from its present location, but if the gap needs changing, move the tracing paper over the top until the two letters look the correct distance apart, then trace off the second letter (as in Version 2 below). Continue the process, choosing alternative letter versions where necessary and opening or closing misjudged gaps. Here, a birthday card has been created using this method (below and right).

Version 1: in this example, the words to appear on a birthday card have been written, but the spacing between the first four letters of 'Happy' is smaller than the spacing between the other letters.

Version 2: on tracing paper: the letter spaces on 'Birthday' have been reduced, to match those in 'Happy'. The 'y' on happy has not been completed so that its final length can be chosen now that 'Birthday' has been finished. A square has been drawn around the lettering for this card to mark the limits of the design feature.

Version 3 completed: the flourishes have been added and the 'y's finished. Hopefully, when this version is traced on to the greetings card, the letters can be spaced with even greater accuracy.

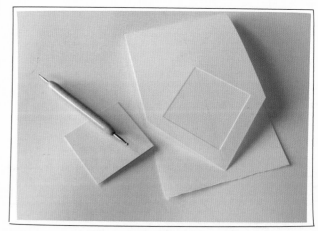

Card for the finished job should be a pale colour and not too thick, so medium-weight watercolour paper works very well. This greetings card has been made with a matching embossed 'platemark' where the words will fit (see 'Creating Platemarks' on page 24).

The greetings card or scrapbook page is placed and aligned over the top of the tracing-paper copy and, with the aid of a light-box, the lettering is traced onto the card. The back lighting shows where to draw the final versions of the letters, achieve even margins and so create a perfect result.

Decorate the card to taste. Here, contrasting insert paper and a tassel have been added to complete the card.

Spacing Words Without a Light-box

You can letter directly on the front surface of a card or page without using a light-box, but it can still be useful to write the words first on a piece of scrap paper to discover how much space they will take up. This is then folded, if necessary, and held under the final destination so that it is possible to see where each letter should be written. If there are two lines of writing, write the lowest one first. Measure the size of space between the right-hand edge of the card and the last letter (below left) done in finger widths, then use the same measurement to position the first letter on the top line (below centre).

Write the lowest line first and measure the distance from the card edge.

Start the top line the same distance from the left-hand edge.

The finished card.

Layout and Design

When writing a verse over several lines, spacing of writing is very much a matter of personal taste, but the advice in this chapter will help you to achieve a pleasing result.

Spacing Lines of Writing

A different atmosphere and emotion can be conjured up by changing the space between lines of writing and altering the space between words. When writing solely in capitals, lines of words can be packed so close together that the space between them is minimal or non-existent. This is a common way of presenting a text in all capitals that covers several lines and is a layout ploy that is worth considering. If lines are spaced too far apart, each appears unconnected but, when letters have ascenders and descenders, collisions are possible, so widening the spaces between lines is the easiest way for beginner calligraphers to avoid this happening.

When words are dense, we feel that we are part of the action. With all these things in close proximity, there's a built-in drama and importance to them.

When line spacing is widened, there is a much more airy feeling, which is dream-like and whimsical.

Another way of discovering a pleasing layout and avoiding collisions is to write the words on scrap paper, cut them out (or the lines of writing), shuffle them around and then tape them or stick them on to a thin backing sheet to taste (right). By squinting, the words appear more dominant than the cut edges of the paper, and the end result is easier to predict. The finished version can be traced off on thin paper, vellum or tracing paper for use, or on to thicker paper or card with the aid of a light-box. Pages 158–9 show you how to attach vellum and tracing paper into a card so that adhesive does not show – techniques that can also be used when using other papers to make cards.

Experimenting with laying out lines of words.

Analysing calligraphy you admire

Pleasing spacing between lines of writing can be discovered by analyzing good-quality images of ancient manuscripts, calligraphy on the Internet, or in books that have examples that you can photocopy. The final appearance of a piece of work will also depend on the length of lines of writing, so if your lines are much shorter than those of the model you like, you may have to make a small adjustment (probably by closing the interline spacing a little). You will often see stunning illustrations where lines of writing are not straight (see below) and you will find that experimentation will provide a wealth of alternatives and opportunities to be creative.

Original size of the manuscript.

From an enlargement, the width of the nib that was used is marked.

The paper template is then used to measure the height of the writing and the line-spacing in nib-widths.

Not all writing has to be on straight lines. Be creative!

Spreading Out Words: Centring

When you want to layout and perfectly centre several lines of writing, first carefully write each line of words on a sheet of spare paper, then measure its length and mark the centre (below left). This may be perfectly adequate for most of your needs, but sometimes – particularly when lines are close together and there are ascenders and descenders filling the spaces between some of them – the gaps between lines can look uneven and another technique is required. This present copy then has to be regarded as an intermediate copy and, in a similar fashion to the method of arranging words described in the previous chapter, the paper is cut through where the lines look too close together, and separated (below right).

Mark the centre of each line.

Hold the mark under a centre line and copy the text.

Correcting the line spacing.

With much love
on your
Birthday

The finished version.

Using a Computer-generated Font to Aid Layout

An alternative, 'cheat's way', to derive the ideal layout is to type the words into a word-processing computer program using a type-font that is similar to the calligraphy style that will be written, and then trace over the printed version. For example, underscored *Lucida Calligra* font is a possible aid for writing in Italic. For the best calligraphy, however, one needs to be well practised in a style before trying this because, as shown below centre, typed letter spacing is never as perfect as calligraphy should be and the copy is only a helpful guide.

Similarly, the letter shapes are never identical to those of a calligraphy style, so one cannot blindly trace from the typed and printed copy. Scribes may prefer to make Italic 'c' and 'e' less rounded than the *Lucida Calligra* versions, the tops of ascenders a different shape and the tail of 'y' wider.

The aim is always to write perfect calligraphic letters with perfect spacing. If a 28pt underscored letter size in this font is used as rough spacing and slope guide for using a ¹⁄₁₆in (1.5mm) wide calligraphy nib (drawing letters down to the underscore line), the lines of writing are likely to be very close in length to those that have been typed. However, each calligrapher's version of Italic is slightly different from that of others – perhaps slightly more compressed, or wider, for example – so experiments are necessary to find what is truly the nearest ideal font size for use with, this or other commonly used nibs.

If a space needs to be filled or increased because calligraphed and typed letters do not match exactly, and some written letter positions have been moved slightly, increase or minimize the length of entry or exit strokes to make spacing look even (bottom right).

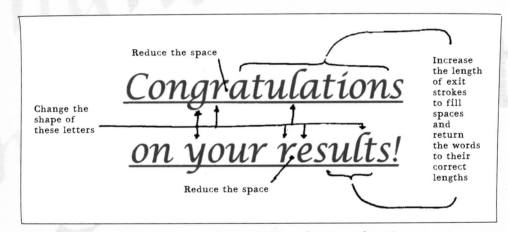

Although *Lucida Calligra* font can be used as an aid to spacing, the space under an 'r' is nearly always too large.

Tracing and adjusting the letters with the aid of a light-box.

The finished card interior. The entry and exit strokes have been adjusted to correct the spacing.

Balancing a Layout

'Balance' refers to the visual appearance of the layout of a page, or the placement of words and other features within an area. Apart from a centred layout, which is obviously balanced, there is no infallible measurement or guide technique for the more irregular positioning of words and decorative features.

When adding a title or short line at the top and another short line at the bottom, the left-hand edge of the top line and right-hand end point of the bottom line are often influential in the final impact. It can be easier to create a more pleasing result if they are staggered and the bottom line is written before adding the title, top line, or top greeting (below left and right).

Off-centre.

Balance at the top.

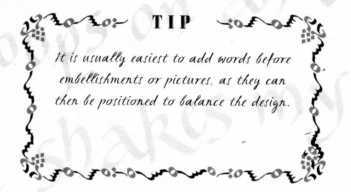

TIP

It is usually easiest to add words before embellishments or pictures, as they can then be positioned to balance the design.

'Framing' the lettering

When positioning other elements, or establishing borders, a frame can help to achieve the best-balanced layout within a defined area, as described on page 26. A clear plastic ruler can also be useful when trying to average out line-ending positions optically, to determine what appears to the eye to be the edge of the writing (right). This will then allow the work to be trimmed with even margins on both sides.

Determining the apparent edge of the writing.

Margins

The size of margins will ultimately be determined by personal taste but, traditionally, most book pages and pictures have been planned with equal top and side margins and a larger one at the bottom, and this is still most people's visual preference (below left).

An alternative option is to make the bottom margin twice the top one and the side margins three-quarters of the bottom one (below right). Recently, however, there has been a trend among picture framers and card designers to make margins equal on all sides (bottom).

Traditional layout, with equal margins top and sides, and a larger margin at the bottom.

Bottom margin is twice the top one and the side margins three-quarters of the bottom one.

Equal on all sides.

Intersecting Thirds

If you analyze attractive or dynamic paintings, or the composition of photographs, you will usually find that your vision is attracted to one feature in particular. In landscapes, horizons are commonly arranged to be one-third of the distance from the top to the bottom of the work, or bottom to top. Portraits are cropped so that the subject's eyes are one-third of the way down from the top. Trees or flowers that attract our attention in pictures are often aligned on one of the imaginary lines one-third of the horizontal distance from a side. So too, the optimum position for placing a dominant feature on a card or page is on an intersection of measured or estimated third lines, top to bottom and side to side (below right).

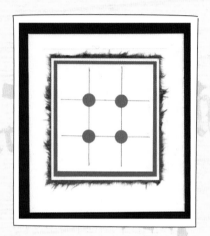

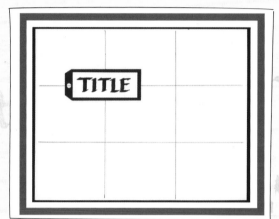

The strongest points on a card or page are where third-lines intersect, so this is the ideal place for a title on a page, whatever the format, although any of the intersections could have been chosen here.

Dominance

As shown below, dominance, or making something stand out in a piece of writing, can be created in various ways: by letter size, colour, weight or density.

Thank you for being a **friend** when I needed one most

Dominance by contrasting the size of letters.

Thank you for being a friend when I needed one most

Dominance by colour.

Thank you for being a **friend** when I needed one most

Dominance by weight. The writing is the normal letter height but uses a wider nib than usual.

Thank you for being a friend when I needed one most

Dominance by pigment density.

96

If you have more than one dominant feature, however, the impact of each is diminished, while impact is enhanced by placing the dominant element on a 'third' line in addition to another characteristic that makes it eye-catching (below).

Free to relax Enjoying our

RETIREMENT

Gardening · Fishing · Visiting friends · Holidays · Walks in the park · shopping · getting up later · Midday concerts · Art gallery Time with grandchildren · Picnic · Cycling · Movies · Boating

The title 'Retirement' stands out because many techniques have been used to make it dominant.

Writing on Curves

Both beginners and those with experience find it difficult to make letter spaces look even when writing on tight curves, so it is advisable to start by only writing on gentle curves.

The guide lines for gently curved writing can be drawn freehand, with French curves, or by cutting a piece of cardboard to a suitable shape and then drawing along its edge. You do not need a compass and should judge the letter spacing 'by eye' and, if you are feeling confident, you may only need a bottom line.

Alternatively, you can just imagine there is a line drawn and let the words wander as you write – an approach best used when the exact position of words is not critical. However, if you keep your writing hand anchored in one place, and your pen at a constant angle on your table top or writing board, then twist and turn and swivel the writing paper as you write, it is quite easy to write on curves without guide lines, providing you're not too fussy about exactly where the writing and curves go. Try it with your normal handwriting!

When using some calligraphy styles, spaces that open up between letters written on curves with a small radius can be partially filled by elongating top or bottom entry or exit lines, and shortening them where letter parts need to be closer together than normal (below left).

If writing around a circle, it is easy to draw in some radius lines from its centre to help you keep the letters on the correct slope – letters should line up with radii. Do not attempt to distort letter shapes until you have had many years of practice. It is much easier to produce a pleasing result by drawing each letter with its normal shape (below right).

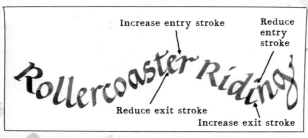

It is not always necessary to draw guide lines for curved writing.

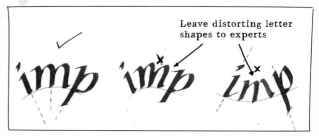

Imagine each letter lined up on a radius to the curve at that point.

The easiest way to create curved lines of writing, stretching from left to right, is to keep all letters vertical and only alter their base position.

The calligraphy here was written using compass-drawn guide lines, then scanned and emailed to a friend, Candy Geeter, who designed the card.

Using words to make borders and pictures

After you have had fun and gained skill by writing on gentle curves, you may like to try using words to make borders with tighter curves (below left), or to create word pictures (below right). You will, however, certainly need guide lines for tight curves in corners, either drawn using a plastic template with a range of hole sizes cut in it, or a compass.

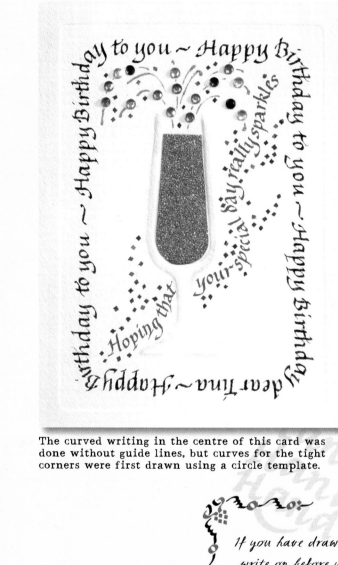

The curved writing in the centre of this card was done without guide lines, but curves for the tight corners were first drawn using a circle template.

Here, words are used to make a design for a festive card.

TIP

If you have drawn a curved guide line to write on before you start lettering, you could also pencil in imagined radii as letter-slope guides in lots of places along its length, which will look like sleepers on a railway track.

PART THREE

Simple ways to make letters special

Creative Letters

Artistic and impressive lettering can be created for cards and scrapbook pages by simple additions and techniques. In this chapter there are a few ideas to experiment with, once you can confidently draw letter shapes in at least one of the basic alphabets in the book.

Decorate

A simple, fun alphabet can be created by writing Italic, Celtic or Roman letters with a fine pen and adding cartoon faces to decorate (see below). An amusing touch could be to customize the faces to look like the recipient of a card or note.

The decorative alphabet below left was written using a wide calligraphy nib and the spirals were added to the letters afterwards, using a fine fibre-tip pen. It is very effective, but a lot harder to master than you might imagine. You will, however, find it easier if you are already used to writing with a calligraphy pen, and if you turn the paper around when necessary to draw the thin lines at the correct angles. The thick strokes should be the same thickness all the way round the curves and the widest lines the pen will draw, so you have to twist your wrist as you pull the pen around each bend. Standing up to write and twisting your body might also help you to draw letters in this style, but you could also draw them as outlines with any writing or drawing implement, fill them in and decorate them to your taste (below right).

These Italic letters could be re-designed to look like someone you know.

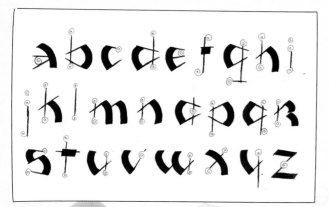

This fun alphabet has been written with many wrist and pen twists.

A decorative card using the fun alphabet.

Wet to wet

For this technique, you add new colour to wet paint. With a wide pen (such as a Speedball C Series nib) write in watery watercolour or gouache paint and then, with a brush, add small amounts of other colours into the wet areas (below left and right).

Practise first, to check that the added paint is the right strength to blend and swirl pleasingly, then create the letters pen stroke by pen stroke, keeping the work flat as you do this. The colours can be added in random or specific places on the letters using fine brushes.

Watery paint added to wet paint will spread and blend.

The blending and final result is never totally predictable.

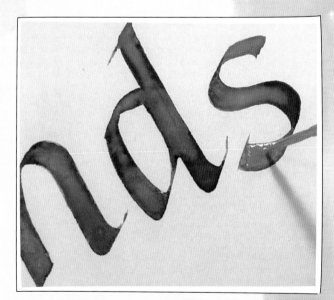

Each letter is written and blended before writing the next one. The blue paint on the bottom of the 's' has dried too much for the paint to blend in swirls, but more blue could have been added to the top of the wet green.

Title for a scrapbook page, ready for pictures, journaling and embellishments.

Blended, or 'striped' letters

If you fill a wide pen, such as a parallel pen, with paint or ink, then touch the side of the nib using a similar pen with a contrasting colour in it, the colours will blend in the centre, but may stay near to their original colours at the edges. This will result in letters with colour 'stripes'. You can also try this technique with a wide Coit pen or Speedball Steel Brush, probably using a brush to add the second colour (below left). Depending on the pen and colours used, the separation of hues may only last for a small number of letter strokes. If you want to use this technique for reasonably consistent colours in all letters, it may be necessary to keep rinsing your nib, drying it and starting again.

When using a normal dip-nib, you can add one colour at the tip and another behind it. As the first colour runs out there will be a little mixing and then the second colour will appear. For a gradual blending, keep adding more paint while there's still some left in the nib, but be careful not to overload it. For example, Alizarin Crimson and Ultramarine Blue will show unmixed as striking pure colours and blend to produce rich purples, or blue and white or blue-green and yellow-green can be blended to make subtle and more monochromatic works.

Very dilute paint can be used at the beginning of a piece of writing and gradually more pigment added for each new line, or you can start with a dense pigment and add more water for new lines or words. Experiment – see what happens if you let each line of writing dry before overlapping it with the next, or just keep writing.

Adding a different colour to one side of the nib.

Creating colour bands in large letters.

A notched balsa-wood pen, loaded with a different colour applied to each section, achieves a clearer separation. The colours will mainly stay separate, but the tip will pick up a mixture of colours where letter strokes cross.

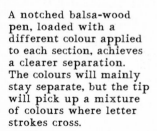

The Italic heading 'Zoo', written with a notched balsa-wood pen contrasts well with the background journaling in Celtic style.

Colour blending, achieved by adding a different watercolour hue to a dip-nib before the previous colour has run out.

Adding more pigment or water to the writing fluid produces varied strengths of colour. Here, the colour was Payne's Grey watercolour. (See also 'Dominance', page 96.)

Multi-media

When a letter drawn with a wide nib has dried, other colours can be added in any of a range of media. A mixture of pens, gouache paint and coloured pencils was used for the lettering below.

Highly textured paper

Writing with a wide nib on highly textured paper, such as 'rough' watercolour paper, can produce letters with character and sparkle, created by the areas of the paper that the colour does not reach.

A decorative, textured element is added by the rough paper showing through the paint.

This multi-media lettering would make an attractive title for a scrapbook page.

Raised, Embossed Letters

For this technique, letter-shaped holes are cut into template card and letters with an impressive, sculpted look are produced by bending thickish paper around the template. The embossing tool has to squeeze between the edges, along with two thicknesses of paper, so make sure that the letters are at least 1in (25mm) high and that the narrowest part of the letter strokes is not too thin.

To cut the curved parts of letters, hold the knife blade in one place on the mat, pointing so that it is comfortable to pull it with your fingers towards the palm of your hand when cutting. Twist the card with the design on it around under the knife point, so the letter outline is continually aligned with the blade, and make lots of very short cuts. Turn the card, not your knife.

CREATING
RAISED LETTERING IN A SUNKEN PANEL

YOU WILL NEED:
Template card (e.g. from shoebox or cereal packet)
¼in (5–6mm) wide Parallel pen, Speedball C Series or other broad nib, two pencils fixed together or similar
Sharp craft knife
Thin paper and glue

1. Write the chosen words onto your template card, using your selected implement (see choice above). Beware of making the narrowest part of the letter strokes too thin, as the embossing tool has to squeeze in between the edges, along with two thicknesses of paper.

2. With the sharp craft knife, cut around the letter shapes and remove them. They will later be discarded but, if any of the letters has an enclosed counter-shape, such as the inside of a 'D', that must be retained. The template card and insides of letters will be glued on to thin paper, in reverse, to hold the parts together.

3. It may be easiest to reposition a counter-shape by relocating the unglued letter in the space. If the letters of the word do not have detached counters or parts that need holding in place, it is not necessary to glue the template to thin paper backing.

{1}

{2}

{3}

4. Trim the edge to ensure a balanced border on the completed embossed card or page, then hold the template against a backlit smooth surface – a window pane or light-box – so that the lettering appears in reverse. If the template has been glued to thin backing paper, the backing paper goes against the lit surface and the top surface of the finished paper rests against the template.

First, use an embossing tool or thick knitting needle around the edge of the template to help hold the finished card or paper in place and create the platemark before embossing the letters.

Be aware that, if the template card is particularly thick and the card or scrapbook's material is thin, it is possible to tear this while bending it and stretching it around the shapes.

Embossing the letters.

The finished card.

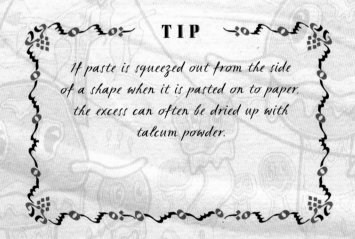

Note

You can use the template time and time again, so later, if you just want to emboss a single letter that appears on one of your old templates, you could put any piece of paper over that template and just emboss that letter on the corner of a page, a luggage tag, greetings card or whatever. You don't have to draw round the edge of the template to create a sunken panel – you could just emboss the letters if you wish.

TIP

If paste is squeezed out from the side of a shape when it is pasted on to paper, the excess can often be dried up with talcum powder.

Embossing other shapes

A different dimension can be added to a card or page by adding other embossed background shapes appropriate to the occasion: footprints or sandcastle shapes would be effective for a beach scene on a scrapbook page, while for a country scene, embossed leaves and branches would make an attractive addition.

Embossing inside holes in the template card creates designs that rise, and embossing around the outside of shaped template card produces sunken shapes when the finished work is turned over to its proper side.

Embossed paw marks add a new dimension to this card. Paw pad-shaped holes were cut in the template card instead of letter shapes.

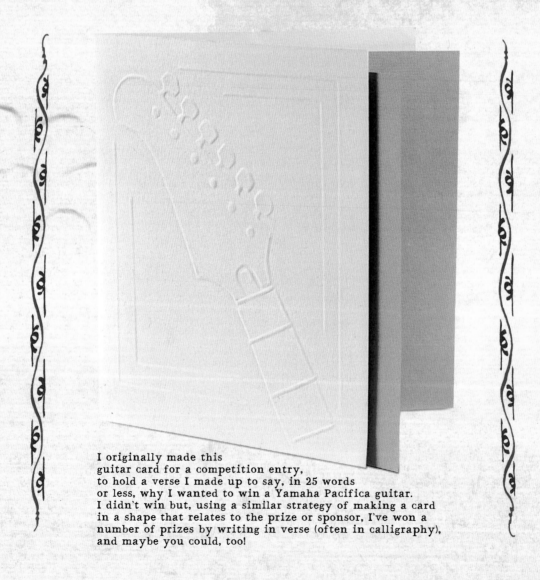

I originally made this guitar card for a competition entry, to hold a verse I made up to say, in 25 words or less, why I wanted to win a Yamaha Pacifica guitar. I didn't win but, using a similar strategy of making a card in a shape that relates to the prize or sponsor, I've won a number of prizes by writing in verse (often in calligraphy), and maybe you could, too!

Pop-up Letters

Simple letter shapes – but with slightly changed proportions – are best for pop-up cards, so that extra thickness is given to horizontal elements, such as the central bar of 'B' and 'H', where the letters will be folded. The cards usually consist of at least two layers, one for the outside of the card and a fractionally smaller inner one for the pop-up letters, which are cut before attaching the two layers.

The alphabet below is particularly suitable for pop-up cards, as the letters are designed to be centrally folded. The letters are based on Italic capitals, but strokes have been widened in places and block serifs added, both to allow for creasing and to keep the end result strong. You can copy them, or make up your own designs in any style you wish.

For all pop-up alphabets, it is important to note that the pointed areas inside 'M', 'N', 'V' and 'W' do not cross the mid-line. The hard lines will be cut right through the layer (throw way the insides that fall out of letters, like the little triangle of 'A' and the middles of 'B', 'D', 'O' and other letters). The broken lines show where the letters will be folded.

Note

If making up your own pop-up alphabet, bear in mind that the letters should be at least ¾–1in (20–25mm) high, or they will be very hard to cut.

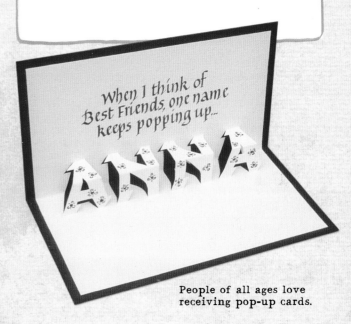

People of all ages love receiving pop-up cards.

ABCDEFGHIJ
KLMNOPQR
STUVWXYZ

A suitable alphabet for pop-up cards.

TO MAKE
A POP-UP CARD

This attractive technique can look very effective and adds a fun and surprise element to any card. The results are impressive, but the technique is not difficult if you follow these instructions.

YOU WILL NEED:
Card (see step 1, below)
Craft knife with pointed blade
Ruler
Scoring tool or knitting needle
Glue stick or double-sided tape
Bone folder or spoon

1. Choose the materials you will use for the inner and outer layers – both will probably be about the same thickness – normal card-making stock. To start with, you will only work on the inner layer.

2. Most pop-up lettering will be only a small number of words. Make a good estimate of how much space these will take up and cut the card a little larger so that it can be trimmed after the letters have been drawn or cut. The height of this inner layer must be at least twice the height of the letters, or they'll stick out of the front of the card when it is closed.

3. Fold the material for the inner layer in half and crease it, making sure that the grain runs along the fold. Bend it backwards and forwards along this crease a few times so that it opens and closes easily, then open it completely and lay it flat again. Draw pencil guide lines an equal distance above and below the fold and draw your letters between them.

4. Cut the edges of the letters (along the solid lines, if using the alphabet provided) fractionally past the guide lines, using a craft knife with a pointed blade.

5. Turn the card over and measure guide lines the same distance from the crease on this side. This is where you score the tops and bottoms of the letters, using a wide knitting needle, embossing tool or anything similar. Check again that the letter cuts extend a tiny fraction past the lines and score marks.

6. Trim the layer so that there is an equal amount of space before and after the lettering, and erase all guide lines. At this stage, add any decoration or extra wording you want on the inside.

7. With the letters on the inside, fold this layer together very slowly and carefully, encouraging the letter-folds to bend forwards, in the opposite direction to the layer fold. Give the centres a gentle push from the back with the scoring tool, and rub the top and bottom letter creases if necessary. Crease the top and bottom dashed lines back, away from you (valley folds) and the central dashed lines forward, towards you (mountain folds).

8. Now create the slightly larger cover so that the lettered layer fits inside with a narrow but even border showing. If you want to emboss a platemark on this, as shown here, do so before sticking the layers together (see Creating Platemarks, pages 24–5).

Attaching the outer and inner layers is described on pages 112–113.

{1}

{2}

{3}

{4}

{5}

{6}

{7}

{8}

The finished card, showing the cover and the separate inner layer.

Have a SCARY Halloween

Attaching the outer and inner layers

1. With the letters now folded inwards on the insert layer, lay it in its final position inside the outer cover, both layers now closed as they will be in an envelope. Open the top layer (the front outside of the card) but leave the bottom three layers (the back of the card and the folded insert) flat on the table, making sure the inside and outside cards do not move relative to each other. Using a glue-stick or double-sided tape, apply a strip of adhesive close to the outer edge of the inner card, which has the lettering on it, and another about halfway in towards the fold (but never closer than two-thirds of the distance).

2. After closing the top layer on to the adhesive, rub it down to make sure it is fixed.

3. If using something hard like a spoon, a sheet of paper should be laid over the card first to prevent shiny marks appearing.

4. Turn the card over so that it is flat on the table, with the new top layer (the back of the card) opened and apply adhesive again to the outside half or two thirds of the inner layer in two strips. This time only partially close the outer layer – just until it is vertical and at right-angles to the table top.

5. Now bring the second glued inner surface up to meet the outside layer, keeping the first two layers flat. Keep the card open at a right-angle while you rub it to fix the two layers strongly and let any glue dry. The sides of the card will always be a fraction convex when it is closed, but this method will ensure that it opens optimally.

The outside front of the card can now be embellished in whatever style you fancy.

TIP

When two layers of card are attached and opened together, there is always tension in the fold, tending to open up a space. The card will open more easily if you allow this to happen and do not try to glue the layers completely.

{1}

{2}

{3}

{4}

{5}

The outside of the completed card, with embellishments added.

Trick or Treat?

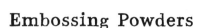

Embossing Powders

Writing with embossing ink pens and covering the wet ink with embossing powder is also highly effective. For an even more decorative effect, background colour can be added before or after the embossed lettering and additions have been completed, and colours can easily be added inside letters that have been drawn as outlines (see facing page).

USING

 # EMBOSSING POWDER

Here, a previously created, blended watercolour background that is dry has been used (see Creative Backgrounds, pages 120–129).

YOU WILL NEED:
Embossing ink pen
Embossing powder
Heat gun or toaster

1. Draw the lettering with an embossing ink pen.

2. Immediately sprinkle embossing powder on each letter, while it is still wet. It doesn't matter what colour of ink is used when opaque powder is applied. Transparent powder over red ink produces raised red letters – but pencil lines drawn as guides could show through.

3. Tap the artwork on to a sheet of paper to remove the excess powder (it can be returned to the stock bottle). In this example, more powder is needed on the corner of the 'h'.

4. Melt and raise the embossing powder, either with a purpose-designed heat gun, like the one shown here, or by holding the paper over a toaster.

5. Once the lettering has been raised, watery colour can be painted over the top of it, and it will run off.

6. Colour can be added and blended inside the hollow letters.

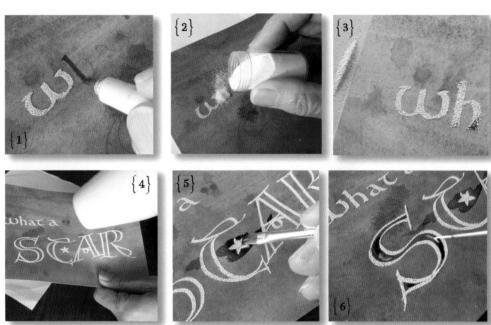

Finished artwork ready to be fixed to a page and have further additions.

Resists

By writing or drawing with resists, you can create light colour letters on a darker background and achieve a dramatic and pleasing effect. Art masking fluid, or Permanent White gouache and waterproof ink are two methods of resist.

Art masking fluid

This milky-looking rubber-based solution, with a smell of ammonia, dries rapidly. It can easily clog fine brushes, so many people apply it with a stick, knitting needle, rounded tip of a pen handle or similar, or a cheap stiff brush. You can also write with it in Automatic pens and Speedball nibs, for example, but they will need cleaning after every few letters. When using this substance and all paint is dry, the masking can be rubbed and pulled to remove it.

USING
ART MASKING FLUID

Be prepared for some frustration – if letter strokes cross and one has partially dried, the second one can lift the first.

YOU WILL NEED:
Art masking fluid
Ink or watery paint

1. Apply the masking fluid resist substance first, and then leave until completely dry.

2. Apply ink or watery paint over the top.

3. Add further layers of resist and colour, if you so choose.

4. When the previous stages have been repeated as many times as desired, and all is dry, peel off the resist, to reveal the lettering.

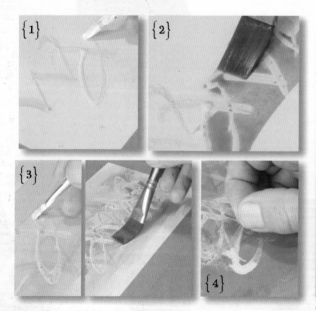

The finished artwork, used on a scrapbook page.

Permanent White gouache and waterproof ink

Alternatively, you can write with a generous amount of Permanent White gouache paint in a dip-nib. When this has completely dried, rapidly apply waterproof ink over the top. After that has dried, more writing or marks can be made with the white gouache, and when that has dried, a different colour of ink can be brushed over the top.

When this layer of ink is dry, the paper is washed in water to soften the gouache, which, if necessary, can be encouraged to become detached by gentle rubbing with a finger tip or perhaps stroking gently with a brush with stiff bristles. Do not expect perfect separation of colours – a little may leak through the gouache. The end result cannot be predicted with certainty.

Here, the paper has been washed to remove the gouache and some of the ink, and some colours have run a little.

Cut Letters

Cut-out letters give an extra dimension to the surface on which they are used, and can provide a striking contrast to smaller writing used for journaling on scrapbook pages. They are particularly effective for titles, but can also be used for short words on greetings cards.

One way of constructing these, so that reasonably-sized letter-shaped holes are left in the page or card stock, is to write with a pen about ½in (12mm) wide or more (e.g. a Speedball Steel Brush, Automatic or Coit pen, or a balsa-wood pen that produces wide letter strokes) and then cut around the edges with a sharp and pointed craft knife (with a cutting mat or thick cardboard underneath) and remove the letters. Any counter areas from letter centres should be kept, and the sheet/page attached to a contrasting coloured background or a photograph, along with the counters if you like complete-looking letters. Alternatively they can be omitted and the spaces outlined in colour or stitching added through the centre of each stroke – either drawn, or actually sewn or machined, if you wish (see below).

With extreme care, very intricate shapes can be cut to produce decorative letters or backgrounds. This example by Sara Burgess could be the initial of someone's name and would make a wonderful gift to be framed, or a very elegant cover of a card. Similar designs of cut letters could also be used to start a title on a scrapbook page, and these would show up best if a contrasting colour of card was fixed behind the holes.

Outlining letter-shaped holes can add interest and make the shapes stand out.

These chunky, decorative Versals by Peter Lloyd, derive from the Middle Ages. The shapes were drawn on coloured mount-board, then the letters cut out using a sharp craft knife and wording added as decoration. Stuck on to a folded backing, they make effective cards for friends.

For inter-connecting letters, remember that the more connections you can make, the stronger the finished cut-out will be. This pointed Italic style has many joining strokes, so is particularly suitable. The letters were drawn by Peter Lloyd with a wide pen, traced onto thin card, then cut out from the front with a sharp scalpel. A 3-dimensional effect was achieved by sticking double-sided tape to both sides of board offcuts, cutting out narrow strips and sticking them to the reverse side of the words, where the letters are broadest. The lettering was then positioned on mounting board and stuck in place.

Although Sara Burgess
has designed and cut
this concertina book
to contain the whole
alphabet, a shorter
zig-zag card could be
created the same way,
or you may wish to
make up simpler
designs for the letters.

Fabric letters

Another effective technique is to use fabric, perhaps
remnants from favourite clothing. Write the letters on
mount-board and then cut them to shape. Paint the top
surface with PVA glue, lay the fabric on top and rub down
to ensure it sticks. When the glue is dry, trim the fabric
from the reverse side, using a very sharp craft knife on
a cutting mat. To ensure clean edges, it is important to
apply a lot of pressure while trimming the fabric.

**Fabric-covered letters are an excellent way to remember
a favourite garment.**

Creative Backgrounds

Watercolours and diluted gouache paint in a range of colours can
be added to wet watercolour paper to create stunning backgrounds
for cards and scrapbook pages.

As with any technique that will wet the paper significantly over a large area, it is advisable to stretch the paper prior to making a start, to prevent it buckling.

Stretching paper allows you the freedom to use as much water as you want, when you want and maximizes the chance of the paper staying flat.

STRETCHING WATERCOLOUR PAPER

YOU WILL NEED:
Watercolour paper
Large horizontal board
Gummed paper tape

1. Wet the sheet of watercolour paper in a bath, or tray of water until it is just saturated. The length of time will depend on the thickness of the paper, but about two minutes will be quite sufficient for all but the thickest varieties.

2. Drain off the excess water, then lay the sheet flat in the centre of a larger horizontal board (make sure there are no air bubbles, but don't rub the surface).

3. Next, tape down each edge of the paper with moistened gummed paper tape about 2in (5cm) wide – half on the paper and half on the board.

4. Keep the board flat until the paper is completely dry – bearing in mind that it may take a day. It must dry naturally, so keep it out of the sun and away from heaters. Leave the paper taped to the board while it is worked on.

Only moisten the gummed paper with a sponge as, if it gets too wet, it may be pulled from the board as the watercolour paper dries and contracts.

Half of the tape is glued to the paper, and half to the board.

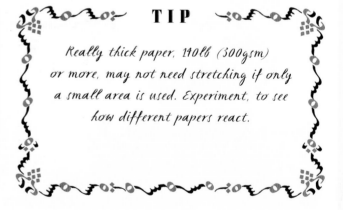

TIP

Really thick paper, 140lb (300gsm) or more, may not need stretching if only a small area is used. Experiment, to see how different papers react.

Blending Colours

Before adding any paint, dampen the stretched paper again with clean water and a sponge. Blend several hues of diluted watercolours or gouaches using wide, soft brushes, and add drips or splodges of other colours on top (right). As the colours contact each other while they are wet, they intermingle and spread. You can leave the result to form by itself, or assist the blending with a brush.

Watery watercolour or gouache paint added to a wet background, so that the colours run.

Adding texture

While the paint is still wet, textures can be added in the following ways:

Crinkled plastic food wrap can be used to dab the surface while the paint is still wet.

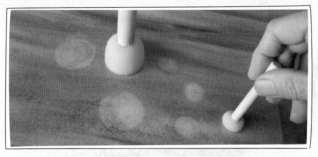

Plain or shaped sponges can be used to add or to remove colour.

Rock salt and table salt can be sprinkled on blended wet watercolours (here, Cobalt blue, Burnt Umber and Sap Green) and the paper left to dry before the salt is brushed off.

Another interesting effect can be achieved by leaving lightly scrunched plastic on the very wet, painted paper until both are dry (left). However, as evaporation is reduced, this may take a while. The effect, after removal of the plastic (right).

Masking with Tape

This is an easy and effective way of blocking off a section of a composition before adding additional paint. Tape is stuck down on a dry surface in the area you want to protect, then painted over as if it wasn't there. The tape protects the area underneath, and when you've finished, you simply pull it off to reveal the design.

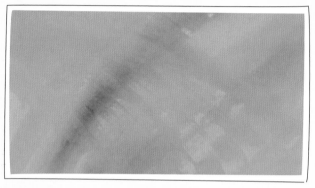

Pale watercolour or gouache paints have been used to create a background layer, which is left to dry. Where pale bands are required, masking tape is then attached.

TIP

To prevent the tape from disturbing the under-layer when it is removed, its adhesive power can be first reduced by dabbing it on to fabric. Experimentation prior to use on the finished work is recommended.

More paint is applied over the masking tape and background, and once this second layer has dried, the masking tape is removed.

The tape is removed very slowly and at a shallow angle. Keep some of the colours to repair any minor damage to the paper.

The nearly finished page, with just a caption and a little journaling still to be completed. Bands are an excellent place for a title and adding other words to a page.

Stencilling

This is another way of masking off an area before applying paint. Stencilling allows for more sophisticated effects than masking tape and for more complex shapes, such as letters, to be cut out. Stencils are usually made from card, as paint and ink can soak through thin paper and drip and run off metal and plastic.

Stencilling has been used to create the lettering and background for this page. The technique is described overleaf.

CREATING
THE STENCILLED EFFECT

YOU WILL NEED:
Watercolour paint
Pencil
Thin card
Blu-Tack
Double-sided tape
Scissors
Fabric (or use the clothes you're wearing)

1. A pale watercolour background was sprayed on to the sheet with a mouth atomizer (but gouache paint or coloured ink could have been used).

2. When this was dry, leaves were temporarily attached with Blu-Tack. A darker colour was spayed over the top, allowed to dry and the leaves removed.

3. Letters for the title were drawn (they could have been traced) in pencil on to thin card and the reverse side covered with double-sided adhesive.

4. After cutting out the letters with scissors and a craft knife, and removing the backing, they were dabbed on to fabric (to avoid permanent adhesion) then stuck on to the background.

5. Another layer of paint was then sprayed over the top and again allowed to dry before the letters were peeled off.

Spraying paint with a mouth atomizer over applied cut letters, which will be removed when the paint is dry.

Note

The cut letters could have been applied at the same time as the leaves or any other features used and the paint could have been or dabbed on with a sponge, or splattered from a toothbrush. When splattering or spraying, it's always best to wear old clothes and work where stray flying paint will not cause damage. Again, experiment before attempting final artwork.

TIP

A number of light layers of paint are better than one thick one, which can drip off the stencilled shapes.

Sponging and Washing

Once writing over a background has been completed, an option is to then remove some of the paint by smudging it with a wet sponge, or remove a large amount by re-wetting the paper and absorbing the disturbed pigment. The words will probably still be visible but be much less dominant (some colours stain the paper more than others). If the paper becomes really soggy, or you choose to take it off the board and put it under the tap to give it a complete wash, it will need to be re-taped to the board while it dries. More colour can then be added and extra lettering drawn.

Here, Cobalt Blue, Sap Green and Burnt Umber watercolours were blended on wet watercolour paper, salt added and the paper left to dry. The salt was removed and the paper re-moistened with a sponge and some of the letters of 'rain' written in Winsor Blue and Payne's Grey watercolours in a William Mitchell's Roundhand dip-nib, so that the colour bled into the paper.

The moist sponge was used to wipe some of the colour from the letters of 'rain' and smudge them to create streaks. When the paper was nearly dry, 'wind' was written using a Speedball C Series nib and the same watercolours. The nib was then rolled in the different colours in the palette and the mixture applied generously, then blown with a drinking-straw.

Paste Papers

This is a fun technique, although it can be rather messy. Coloured paste can be applied to a sheet of paper first then written on with an implement – for example a clothes peg, notched balsa wood, or a knitting needle – while it is wet. Alternatively, for a resist effect, wax crayons, or oil-pastels can be used for writing or creating designs prior to the application of coloured paste.

Note

Recommended papers for this technique include text-weight 28lb (104gsm) Mohawk Superfine; Arches text wove; Canson Vivaldi and Canson Mi-Teintes, and thin hot-pressed watercolour paper, but experiment, as you may find others equally good.

Here, journaling the foods eaten on the picnic was written into the wet paste with a paintbrush handle.

THE PASTE

YOU WILL NEED:
Rice flour
Wheat flour
Steamer or glass bowl in pan
Glycerine and liquid detergent
Matt or gloss acrylic medium
Lidded containers

1. Mix 4 tablespoons of rice flour, 3 tablespoons of wheat flour and 3 cups (1¼ pints/750ml) of water and leave to stand for half an hour or more. Bring gradually to the boil in a steamer, or glass bowl in a pan of water (i.e. not over direct heat) and blend and stir constantly until the mixture thickens, but is still runny enough to pour. If too thick, add more cold water.

2. Stir in ½ a teaspoonful of glycerine and 1 teaspoon of liquid detergent and, when the mixture is cool, 2 teaspoons of matt or gloss acrylic medium.

3. If not for immediate use, separate the paste into lidded containers when cool and store in the fridge, where it should last for a few days.

4. Use tubes of 'school quality' or artist's acrylic paint to add colour, as wanted, bearing in mind that the paste dries a lighter tone. Try about 1 dessertspoonful of paint to half a cup of mixture to start with, but be prepared to add more.

This was written in gouache paint on dried paste paper.

CREATING
A PASTE PAPER

YOU WILL NEED:
Coloured paste mixture (see previous page)
Brush, at least 1½in (4cm) wide
Chosen implement for making patterns
Washing line or newspaper
Boards and weights

1. Wet the paper by dragging it through water, then drain it and sponge it flat on to a laminate table top or acrylic sheet, working outwards to remove excess water, especially from the edges.

2. With a brush at least 1½in (4cm) wide, immediately apply coloured paste to the damp paper, either as a single or a mixture of colours. Brush the paste over the sheet to produce an even and thin layer.

3. Any object that does not break the soft paper surface can then be used to write in the wet paste – maybe a plastic clothes peg (as shown here), a knitting needle, clean calligraphy dip-nib, bamboo cane pen, or piece of balsa wood.

4. Patterns can also be combed – as here, using a piece of notched balsa wood on wet paste paper – stamped, or rolled into the colour to create backgrounds.

5. Experiment and have fun, then hang your paper on the washing line, or lay it flat on newspaper while it dries.

6. Wash all equipment thoroughly as soon as you have finished.

7. Papers usually curl to some extent when they dry, but will flatten if kept in a folder squeezed between books or boards, or stored under a weight, and if necessary, they can be ironed on the reverse side when dry, too.

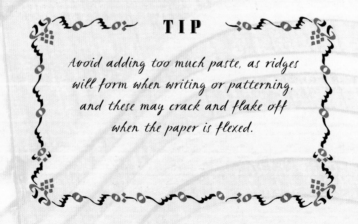

TIP

Avoid adding too much paste, as ridges will form when writing or patterning, and these may crack and flake off when the paper is flexed.

{1}

{2}

{3}

{4}

{5}

{6}

{7}

PART FOUR

Extra ideas for advancing calligraphers

Gold and Silver Ink and Paint

If you want to add brilliance, glamour and sophistication to your artwork, a touch of gold or silver will do the trick. Stunning effects are easy to achieve, but you need to be aware of the possible pitfalls and know how to avoid them.

Although gold and silver inks look bright, they will eventually tarnish and go dull and, because they contain metal particles, they cannot be used with traditional fountain pens.

Gold and silver gouache paint is a popular choice, diluted with water until it just runs freely in the palette, and then loaded in to a dip-nib or a wide pen with a brush, and written with in the conventional way. While gold and silver paint and ink each have their devotees, whichever you use, sedimentation is so rapid that, even while writing, the first marks made by the pen are likely to deposit the most particles and look densest, so the mixture needs frequent stirring and the writing surface must be kept horizontal.

Wide nibs tend to pull metallic particles to the end of writing strokes, resulting in uneven coverage of gold and silver inks and paints. This variation can be attractive or a nuisance. Problems of even coverage are much less obvious when a narrow nib is used.

As well as being used for Copperplate writing, 'Hunt Imperial 101' and similar pointed nibs can be used in a penholder to draw very fine lines for shadow effects around letters using gold or silver ink or diluted metallic gouache, and also for all other paint and ink colours.

As before, the colour is brushed on to the underside of the nib (below left) and test marks made to ensure fine-drawn lines (below centre). If the paint or ink is of the correct consistency, a reservoir is not essential.

Loading a pointed nib with imitation gold gouache paint.

Draw some test squiggles after each pen loading to check the paint or ink flow and the fineness of lines.

Using a pointed nib and gouache paint. Variation in line-thickness can be created, by changing the pressure applied to the nib and the direction in which it is moved.

Gel pens and metallic markers

These are convenient to use and can produce pleasing results, especially on coloured stock, and while the archival nature of the pigments is uncertain and there is a possibility that an oil outline may eventually show around the dried colour lines, the results are likely to last a significant time.

A gold gel pen was used around this letter. In some lights the gold has a pleasing sparkle, but the line width is always constant.

Gold Leaf

Gold leaf is easy to apply and is sold in a range of grades – 24ct gold is pure, but 22 and 23ct will be perfect for cards and scrapbooking. Manufacturers usually package it in books of 25 leaves, each being 3¼in (8cm) square and tucked between protective tissue pages, but some stores and suppliers will sell a single leaf or a 5-leaf book to make it affordable.

Sheets of 'loose' gold leaf, as the name suggests, are simply very thin sheets of gold – so thin that they are easily damaged and apt to blow away in the slightest breeze. A sheet of 'transfer' gold leaf is a sheet of loose gold that has been very lightly attached to a backing paper with pressure or a trace of wax. This makes transfer gold leaf much easier to handle and is the best choice for first attempts at gilding. The sheets – the backing and the gold – can be cut with sharp clean scissors.

All references to gold leaf and descriptions of using gold leaf in this book presume that the reader is using transfer gold leaf (which is sometimes just called 'transfer gold'). A capital letter, small decoration or flower centre that is gilded with it will shine far brighter than any imitation substance, even when the latter is freshly applied.

Note

Pure silver is rarely used for calligraphy because it will oxidize in the atmosphere and tarnish. Platinum leaf and aluminium leaf can be used as a substitute but are thicker and harder to work with than gold leaf. Other metals are also sold in thin leaves for calligraphic use along with a range of 'gesso' glues and instructions for their use.

Transfer gold leaf

To apply transfer gold leaf, you must first write or paint with a 'gesso' – a special form of glue. Beginners will find it much easier to apply the gesso with a fine brush, rather than with a pen. When painting or writing with this glue, aim to create a layer that is slightly domed above the paper or card surface when it is dry. If the stock is absorbent, you may need to apply two layers or to use a brush to add more of the mixture into the wet letter or shape. Gesso can be bought ready-prepared, or you can make it yourself (see facing page). As gold leaf can adhere to paint, it is always advisable to lay it before surrounding colours are added, or with surrounding areas masked off, perhaps by covering them with paper.

When adding picture design elements to a scrapbook page, it is not always necessary to make them realistic. The colourful leaves on this tree with a gold trunk are based on medieval designs. A book of gold leaf (with the purple wrapper) is shown on the right-hand side, along with a silk dusting cloth.

Making gesso

The easiest way to make gesso is to mix PVA glue with about a third to half as much water added – as always, the aim is to make it just thin enough to easily leave the brush or nib. PVA woodworking glue works well, but scrapbookers might prefer to purchase an acid-free variety.

As PVA dries transparent and colourless, a tiny touch of bright red watercolour or gouache paint can also be added to the gesso mixture so that it is easier to see where it has been applied.

Creating a small, domed spot of glue mixture with a vertically held brush. The spot is first produced with the bristles of the brush scraped to a fine point then, while the gesso is still wet, more is added to the top with the brush more heavily laden. The mixture should not spread out past the original outline. It's better to add several small extra amounts, rather than an enormous amount of extra gesso all at once.

TIP

When painting small spots, scrape the brush to a fine point and hold it vertically, with the handle making a "J" shape against your thumb. Keeping the side of your hand on the paper, just touch the point of the brush on the paper for a tiny dot or spot, or use it to draw a very small circle or tight spiral for a slightly larger one.

APPLYING
TRANSFER GOLD

If you are applying gold to a large letter or complex shape, it will be easiest to gild it in sections – the joins will not show.

YOU WILL NEED:
Dried gesso shape
Transfer gold leaf
Silk, or other soft cloth

Gold leaf is incredibly thin and easily detached from the backing sheet, so sometimes a bigger area than intended will flake off when attaching it to gesso. It can also come off on fingers, so keep your fingers off the gold and, as far as possible, only handle it by the small border of backing paper that exists.

If gold attaches itself to paint, it can often be removed with an eraser or by light scraping with a sharp blade.

1. Holding the sheet of transfer gold in one hand, poised with the gold near to the shape and with the work on a cool surface to aid condensation, target four or five long deep breaths at the dried gesso from very close range, to make it slightly sticky.

2. Immediately, push the gold on to the gesso, through the backing paper, with a finger or thumb. A second or two of pressure is all you need.

3. Dust off any surplus gold, preferably with something made of silk (which attracts the gold by static electricity), but any type of very soft cloth can be used, or a paper tissue.

4. The completed gold spot.

If the gold does not adhere completely, it can be applied again. Possible reasons are:

- Insufficient glue/gesso was in place (add some more and let it dry again)

- Not enough breath was expended (or from too far away)

- Time lag was too long before applying gold.

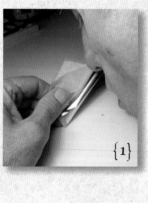

{1}

{2}

{3}

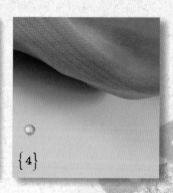

{4}

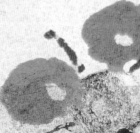

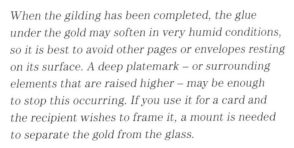

Note

When the gilding has been completed, the glue under the gold may soften in very humid conditions, so it is best to avoid other pages or envelopes resting on its surface. A deep platemark – or surrounding elements that are raised higher – may be enough to stop this occurring. If you use it for a card and the recipient wishes to frame it, a mount is needed to separate the gold from the glass.

Creating flowers

{a}

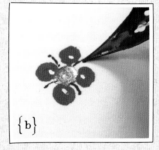

{b}

{c}

The easiest flowers to paint have three or four petals about the same size as the centre spot, and these are touched on to the gold. Wet paint will run off the gold.

Fine stamens can be drawn with the pen nib upside down.

White spots can be added, too (see the Tip on page 135), but they are optional extras – neither these, nor stamens are essential.

Here, the flowers make a decorative feature on this name, which could be used for a scrapbook page title, or for a card.

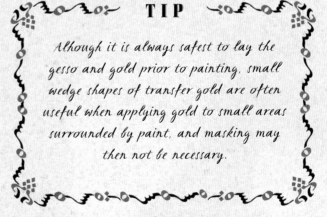

TIP

Although it is always safest to lay the gesso and gold prior to painting, small wedge shapes of transfer gold are often useful when applying gold to small areas surrounded by paint, and masking may then not be necessary.

Drawn and Painted Capitals

When plain or decorated capitals are required – for page titles or initial letters, for instance – one option is to draw outlines and paint the letters, or gild them with gold leaf. Coloured pencils and other media can also be used.

For precision painting, the best brush or brushes you can afford will reward you with the ease they can be used to paint sharp corners and fine lines. The sizes you need depend on the dimensions of letters you wish to construct, but for small letter heights, a pure sable brush in sizes 00 and 1 should be useful. You can add other brush sizes as you feel you need them.

Design for a page title using Roman capitals. The following media were used for the letters (left to right): 23ct gold leaf on PVA, gouache, blended watercolours, ink, watercolour, coloured pencils.

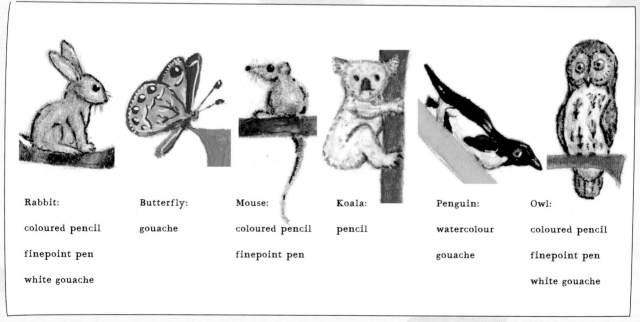

Rabbit:	Butterfly:	Mouse:	Koala:	Penguin:	Owl:
coloured pencil	gouache	coloured pencil	pencil	watercolour	coloured pencil
finepoint pen		finepoint pen		gouache	finepoint pen
white gouache					white gouache

This shows the media used for the individual animals.

Roman Letters

These drawn and painted versions of classic Roman letters are not intended to be practised.

Their proportions and features can be incorporated in capitals of other styles, or they can be copied as required.

ROMAN PAINTED CAPITALS

Versals

Versal letters have their origins in classic Roman letters, but their straightest elements are usually slightly more 'waisted', curved portions are exaggerated and serifs altered. For different effects, you can draw them with a pen or as outlines with other writing and drawing tools and complete them as you choose. In medieval times, large Versals were decorated with pictures in their counter-spaces, given backgrounds filled with gold, a mixture of tiny coloured and gilded squares (diaper backgrounds), or leafy trails added and perhaps incorporated into border designs. The letters, too, often had shading, fine white lines or other detail added. We can borrow some ideas and modernize them, as I show you here.

This fragment from a fourteenth-century manuscript shows a white-lined capital on a gold background and part of a trail.

Original size 2in (5cm) square. A decorative letter like this, or a name on a card, makes a special gift that can be framed, or can start a title or feature on a scrapbook page.

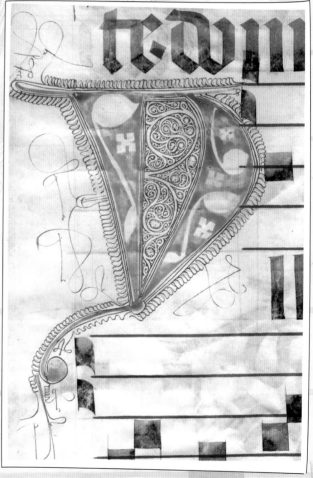

A fragment of an original sixteenth-century manuscript.

The author's interpretations of medieval letters.

The construction of Versals

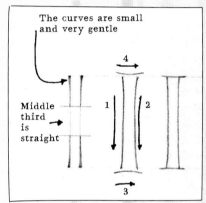

The curves are small and very gentle

Middle third is straight

Straight stokes are only just off parallel, and serifs are added last of all.

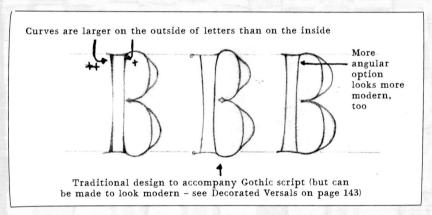

Curves are larger on the outside of letters than on the inside

More angular option looks more modern, too

Traditional design to accompany Gothic script (but can be made to look modern – see Decorated Versals on page 143)

If limbs or curved letter parts are added to a straight element, the straight vertical is constructed to be more hollowed on the outside than the inside.

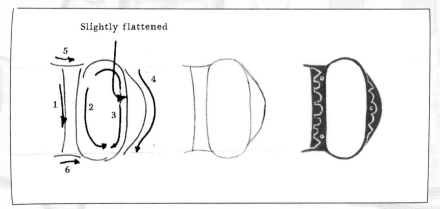

Slightly flattened

The inside of a curve is drawn and flattened, and the outside is then blended on to it. The colouring and decoration possibilities are endless.

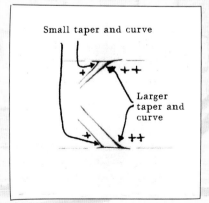

Small taper and curve

Larger taper and curve

More thickness is added to the outside of a serif on a diagonal than on the inside.

VERSAL LETTERS DRAWN WITH A PEN

AaBbCc

DdEeFfGgHh

IiJjKkLlMmNn

OoPpQqRrSs

TtUuVvWvv

SPECIAL NOTES

The space between strokes at the centre is 1 nib-width if leaving the letters hollow and pen-drawn. Letters are 24 nib-widths high

Pen angle is about 0° for verticals and 90° for horizontal letter parts

Pen angle is about 20° for curved strokes

Fill in using the nib's corner, or by twisting the pen

If drawing letters with a very narrow calligraphy nib (you always use one that's much finer than your writing nib), you will need to twist it from vertical to horizontal on some letter strokes. Letters can be left hollow, filled in, or decorated, if wide enough.

DECORATED VERSALS

ABCDEFGHI
JKLMNOPQRS
TUVWXYZ

These decorated Versal letters have more exaggerated proportions, and were originally designed to accompany Gothic small letters. However, by painting, decorating and embellishing them creatively, they can look modern and be used for a wide variety of themes for greetings cards and scrapbook pages. Enlarged capital letters from other writing styles can be given similar treatments.

The shape of these painted Versals gives scope for added decorations inside each letter.

Modern Versals

The modernized versals shown below are designed to be constructed using several pen strokes for most letters, but with slightly less exaggerated proportions than traditional varieties.

They are not easy to draw with a pen but can also be outlined with a pencil and coloured. They can be used for titles and in verses, and also to produce letters suitable for rubbings and other creative purposes.

MODERNIZED VERSALS

ABCDEFGH
IJKLMNOPQ
RSTUVWXYZ

SPECIAL NOTES

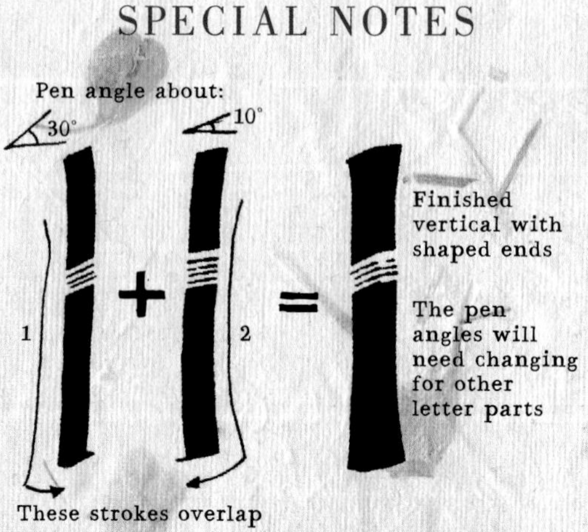

Pen angle about: 30° 10°

1 + 2 =

These strokes overlap

Finished vertical with shaped ends

The pen angles will need changing for other letter parts

 # TRAILS

Trailing and branching stems with leaves, flowers, beasts, birds and bugs are a very traditional way of decorating a page to make the contents look important.

Trails can be drawn as a separate border, or constructed to appear to grow from the side of a large capital letter. All writing and letter painting is completed first, then the trail is drawn in pencil with leaf stalks making 'v' shapes with the stem and pointing back towards the letter. They can be left in pencil or coloured pencil (not black or felt-tip pen), or drawn over with a copperplate nib and watery paint. Flowers and wildlife are then added to taste.

{a}

This trail was sketched in pencil, then gone over with watery paint.

{b}

The leaves have been added, using more transparent, watery paint.

The trail below includes flowers in several shades of pink, with gold gouache centres and similar-sized touching petals. Gold leaf, rhinestones, pearls, dimensional paint or other media could have been used for the flower centres, to add an exotic touch to the trails.

{c}

The final decorations have been added.

{d}

The same trail created only with coloured pencils and 3D punched flowers (see facing page).

Painting techniques for leaves and letters

When painting leaves and letters, scrape paint from the loaded brush until it comes to a fine point, then keep twisting the paper to align the bristles with the line to be painted. Lift the brush off the paper as the tip is pulled out through corners and sharp points (see below). Outline shapes in this way first and then fill in central areas.

{1}

Twist the paper so that the bristles point along the outline.

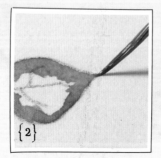

{2}

Raise and pull the bristles out from leaf or letter points.

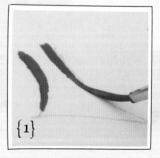

{1}

Drag the brush along outlines.

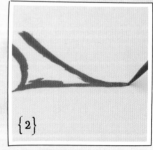

{2}

Paint the outline of a shape first, then fill in the middle.

Paper-sculpted Trails

To construct paper-sculpted trails such as the example below, first trace the trail lines on to the reverse of the paper/card and then support it on a soft pad.

Next, run an embossing tool or ballpoint pen along the lines prior to trimming them to width and adding some leaves and any decorations of your choice.

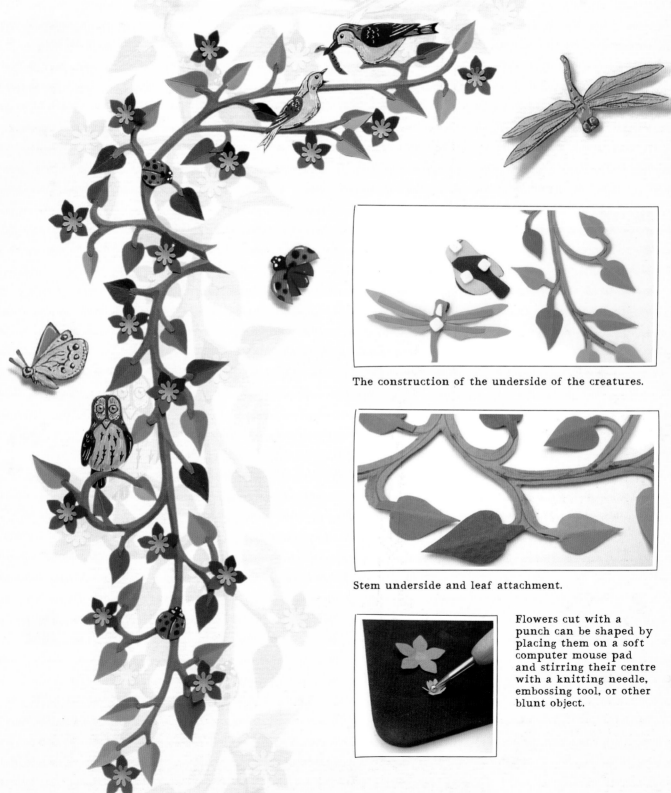

The construction of the underside of the creatures.

Stem underside and leaf attachment.

Flowers cut with a punch can be shaped by placing them on a soft computer mouse pad and stirring their centre with a knitting needle, embossing tool, or other blunt object.

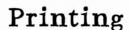

Printing

Print techniques enable multiple copies of a card to be produced in a time-effective manner, and the nature of the end-product can add a new, artistic dimension to the use of calligraphy.

 **RUBBING**

YOU WILL NEED:
Thin cardboard
Thin paper
Crayons, or coloured pencils

When thin paper is placed over a rough surface and blunt points of pencils, crayons or coloured pencils, for example, are rubbed over the paper, the texture or pattern of the surface underneath is revealed. This principle can be used to create prints from raised lettering or cardboard from which letter shapes have been removed.

1. Letters are drawn or written on thin cardboard, then cut out and pasted on to a backing sheet of paper.

2. Thin paper is laid over the design and a mixture of coloured and graphite pencils are used to shade over the design, using the sides of the points.

3. By moving the paper a little after the completion of the first print and repeating the process, overlapping copies can generate an attractive effect.

{1}

{2}

{3}

An alternative method

1. For a different appearance, a word or two can be written on thin card and then the letters removed on a cutting mat, using a sharp craft knife. This template, or printing plate, is glued on to backing paper, too, and areas of card from the counter spaces in letters attached. Unlike a stencil for embossing raised letters, the backing is glued behind the letters so that, when it is laid on a table, the words are the normal way round.

2. Thin paper for the finished work is then laid over the design and rubbed with coloured and graphite pencils. Gold brass-rubbing wax can also be applied effectively to any rubbed lettering.

{1}

{2}

TIP

The most pleasing results are usually obtained by keeping all pencil strokes parallel to each other, but not trying to be neat in other ways. Let the pencils wander over the surface to create patchy colour rather than hard stripes – changes of colour can fill in the gaps – and aim for a ragged edge.

Carving

Letters and designs can be carved in reverse into lino, other printing block material, or vinyl erasers, for printing. It is probably easiest to first write normally, or draw letters on paper and then trace the outline on to tracing paper with a sharp HB or 2B pencil.

When this tracing is turned over and on to the print block material, the graphite is transferred by rubbing the clean side of the sheet with a fingernail, the edge of a spoon or similar, checking to see if the design is showing. The pencil lines may show up more clearly if you first prepare the printing surface by putting abrasive kitchen cleaning powder on a flat surface and rubbing the block over it (and you can also try painting the cleaned surface with white gouache),

but this is not always necessary. Drawing over the transferred design with a ballpoint or permanent ink pen makes it less likely to be rubbed off when the block is handled while it's being carved.

For small designs, particularly on erasers, the printing block can be stamped on to ink pads and then on to the final paper, or ink can be applied to them with brush pens or embossing ink pens. Experiment with several stampings before re-inking and do not expect perfect outlines. Embossing powder can also be sprinkled on to the wet embossing ink and melted if so desired. This makes the word or words more dominant – particularly if contrasted with flat and non-embossed surroundings.

Carving and printing with erasers

Erasers and soft material can be carved with a sharp knife. Aim to make cuts away from the printing surface, so that each letter stroke is at the apex of a ridge with outward sloping sides.

Embossing powder has been used on the third line down of the darker prints, raising the ink and making it shine and stand out.

Carving and printing with lino

Specialist sets of lino tools are usually used to carve lino.

Larger blocks may give the best print quality when artist's quality lino or block-printing ink is rolled on to them with a rubber roller or 'brayer'.

For an even result, once the printing paper is in place, an old spoon can be rubbed over the letters and design to make sure the ink touches the final paper.

The printed linocut.

Printing on wet paste paper

This linocut has been stamped into wet, freshly made, paste paper, a technique that enables multiple prints of words to be created on a single sheet. This can be used to produce a background for a scrapbook page, take the place of the traditional title, to act as a form of journaling, or to create an interesting feature or texture. Printing blocks of all kinds can be used in this way.

PART FIVE

Mass-producing cards

Adding Words on Inserts

If making a large number of identical cards, you may only have time to handwrite the recipient's and your own name on each of them, not the verse or message as well. Here are some time-effective ways to produce professional-looking results.

Printing the Wording

Once the wording for a card has been designed and written, and spacing perfected, multiple copies can be printed and attached, either to the interior as an insert, or to the exterior surface. Parchment papers are widely used as a writing paper for calligraphy, and also for laser and inkjet prints, and for photocopies, but some translucent papers can be printed, too. Depending on the format of the card and, after a combination of measurement and trial and error, it is sometimes possible to arrange several copies of the verse to appear on each printed sheet of paper, with a minimal number of cuts needed to separate them. Making up the printing master can be done in a computer word-processing program, or by 'cut and paste' (see below), prior to rescanning or photocopying.

Master artwork wording.

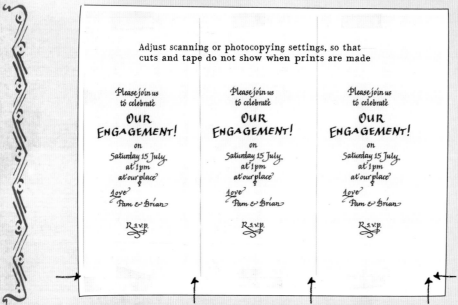

Reduced artwork attached to backing paper the same size as the copy paper. The arrows show where cuts will be made to divide up the printed sheets.

As always, the verse on the master copy should be positioned so that, after printing, trimming and folding as necessary, the grain of the insert paper will align with that of the card. For increased impact, a splash of colour or decoration can be added to inserts that have been printed in black, if time allows. One advantage of generating inserts by such a mechanical printing method is that the original calligraphy can be written larger than the finished version that will appear in the card, and reduced copies attached in appropriate places to produce the printing master. This nearly always makes letters look sharper and small imperfections less obvious – however, if you reduce the work too much, the thinnest letter strokes may break up, so do not to reduce artwork by more than 50%.

Attaching the Wording

Using an insert for words – whether printed for a mass mail-out, or handwritten for a one-off production – allows for error of judgement to be made without ruining the whole card. However an insert is attached, the smaller the area that has adhesive applied to it, the flatter the whole sheet is likely to remain. For example, if the insert remains unfolded, it is probably only necessary to glue the top edge, with a glue-stick, perhaps, or apply double-sided tape to it (see below).

Both the pink backing and printed insert are only attached by adhesive here

Please join us
to celebrate
OUR
ENGAGEMENT!
on
Saturday 15 July
at 1pm
at our place

love
Pam & Brian

R.s.v.p.

An insert attached at the top only.

FIXING
A FOLDED INSERT INTO A CARD WITH ADHESIVE

YOU WILL NEED:
Card
Glue-stick or double-sided adhesive tape

In a folding card, a folded insert can also hide marks made on the inside of the front cover, perhaps resulting from embossing it.

1. The insert should be smaller than the card, so trim it to allow a ³⁄₁₆in (4mm) border around all sides when the card is opened flat.

2. Fold the insert in half and place it in the card in the position it will be attached, its folded edge firmly in the crease of the card, and the card closed around it.

3. Lay the back of the card flat on the table and hold the closed insert in position while the front cover is fully opened.

4. If using a glue-stick, run it only once along the insert fold so that half of it is on the paper of the insert and half on the front cover of the card (top left photograph on facing page). The front of the card is then closed on to the insert and pressure applied to the outside.

5. If using double-sided adhesive tape, attach it first to the inside of the front cover of the card, close to but not touching the crease and with the outer protective covering left in place (top right photograph on facing page).

6. Arrange the insert as previously described, with the card closed and laid flat on its back. Holding the insert closed and ensuring that it doesn't move, raise the front cover. After removal of the protective strip, close the front cover on to the insert (photograph in centre of facing page).

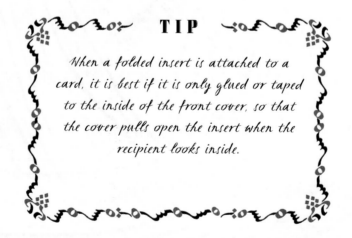

TIP

When a folded insert is attached to a card, it is best if it is only glued or taped to the inside of the front cover, so that the cover pulls open the insert when the recipient looks inside.

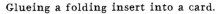
Glueing a folding insert into a card.

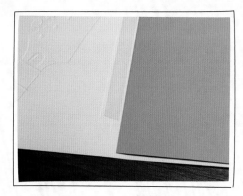
Double-sided adhesive added to a cover.

Closing the cover on to the carefully positioned and held insert.

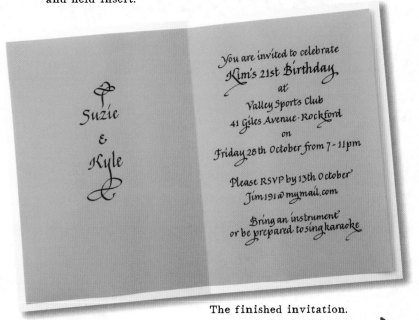

Suzie
&
Kyle

You are invited to celebrate
Kim's 21st Birthday
at
Valley Sports Club
41 Giles Avenue · Rockford
on
Friday 28th October from 7 - 11pm

Please RSVP by 13th October
Jim191@mymail.com

Bring an instrument
or be prepared to sing karaoke

The finished invitation.

A METHOD OF ATTACHING
VELLUM OR TRACING PAPER

YOU WILL NEED:

Tracing paper, with printed or written text

Ribbon

A sharp knife

Adhesive tape (or tiny spot of glue)

Cutting mat

Backing card

1. Attach the tracing paper with a fragment of adhesive tape, then cut two slits for the ribbon that will cover the tape and thread it through both of them.

2. Cross the ribbon on the reverse side, poke the ends back through the slits and pull sideways to tighten the fastening.

3. The finished card. A plain backing with a heart or initials drawn on it to show through, for example, could have been an alternative.

{1}

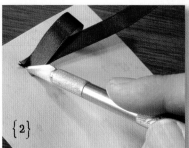

{2}

{3}

Other methods of attachment

While tracing paper and other translucent paper can be printed or written on, glues and adhesive tape applied to these for attachment usually show through. The methods below, which show how to attach these materials to a card without the glue showing, work equally well for attaching standard paper.

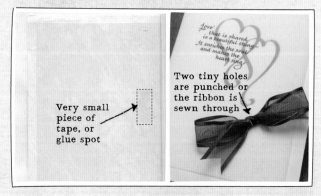

Very small piece of tape, or glue spot

Two tiny holes are punched or the ribbon is sewn through

Attach tracing paper to the outside of the card by fixing at the back first with a tiny piece of tape, or spot of glue. Use ribbon on its own to hold the tracing paper to the front.

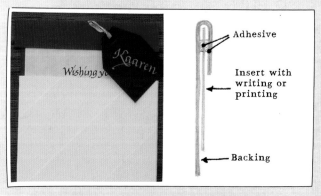

Adhesive

Insert with writing or printing

Backing

Cover the attachment point with a fold of card. This card slides in a sleeve, and is designed to look like a gift (left). Insert the attachment in the fold (right).

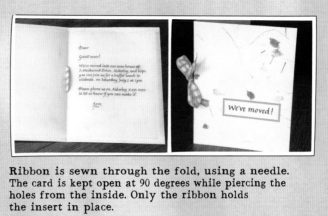

The card is tied with
ribbon passed around the
back and through slits in
the creases and side flaps.
The wheelbarrow on this
card covers the glue used
to attach the tracing paper.

Ribbon is sewn through the fold, using a needle.
The card is kept open at 90 degrees while piercing the
holes from the inside. Only the ribbon holds
the insert in place.

Commercial Printing

If you plan to pay a commercial printer to print your
words in raised or foiled gold, or any special colour,
they will probably prefer you to write in black ink.
Your version will be scanned and converted to make a
printing plate and the ink or foil colour of your choice
will be added to the press. However, technology and
working methods keep changing, so it is best to talk to
printers and discuss their preferences and requirements
before you produce your finished artwork.

Artwork, cast printing plate and the resulting card
with gold-foil lettering.

Purchasing card and paper in bulk

If you plan to make a lot of cards out of the same
materials, the cheapest way to buy paper or card
is often to look through the wholesale catalogues
supplied to your printer, make a selection and ask
the printer to order the amount you need. Full sheets
cost the least, but these can be around 3ft x 2ft 4in
(1m x 70cm) and difficult to handle. For a small extra
cost, you can also have your paper guillotined to size,
by the printer or his wholesaler, but remember to
stipulate which direction you want the grain to run.

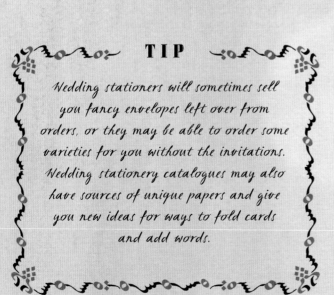

TIP

*Wedding stationers will sometimes sell
you fancy envelopes left over from
orders, or they may be able to order some
varieties for you without the invitations.
Wedding stationery catalogues may also
have sources of unique papers and give
you new ideas for ways to fold cards
and add words.*

Envelope Design for Cards and Scrapbook Pages

The amount of time you spend creating 'mail art' will probably depend on the nature of the occasion and the person to whom a card is being sent.

Personalizing

It is worth bearing in mind that envelopes are less likely to be kept than the card – unless it is very artistic and the recipient is appreciative – and that young children rarely save cards or envelopes, no matter how much effort has been expended.

When mass-mailing to 100 people, it is doubtful that you will have the time to give each envelope the same degree of attention as you would for a one-off special production for a friend or relative, who will treasure it and the contents forever.

However, you can still personalize each envelope a little. A combination of the recipients' initials or highlighted names can be effective (see right), maybe together with a simple decoration in a similar colour to one used on the card inside. A decorative punched hole in the envelope, showing a taste of the card inside, is also attractive (see below). Bear in mind, though, that when used for mailing or covering a card, the envelope should build anticipation for the far more impressive contents – and, if it is going to be handled by a postman, the address needs to be really obvious and very easily read.

An envelope decorated with initials, and a punched hole that shows the card inside.

Emphasizing the recipient's name. The spirals were added with a highlighter.

Home-made Envelopes

As envelopes are only manufactured in a finite range of sizes, and the choice of colour or paper quality is strictly limited, it is always easiest to obtain or choose an envelope before making the card to fit inside. However, if you want to satisfy your creativity by making an envelope out of the same paper as used for a card, or to fit into a scrapbook page theme, the following designs are economic and straightforward to produce. The envelope designs shown overleaf can be altered in many ways by using different shapes and sizes of flaps, so these plans are just to start you thinking. Each envelope looks different from the back, so your preference for the appearance of one or the other may influence your choice.

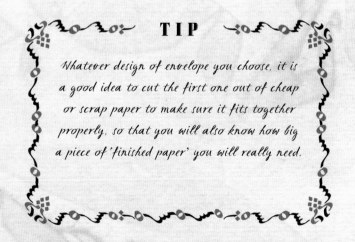

TIP

Whatever design of envelope you choose, it is a good idea to cut the first one out of cheap or scrap paper to make sure it fits together properly, so that you will also know how big a piece of 'finished paper' you will really need.

 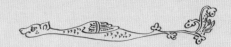

MAKING
ENVELOPES

A design for a home-made envelope

YOU WILL NEED:
Paper
Double-sided adhesive tape
Craft knife
Blunt implement for scoring

1. First, place the card to be enclosed in the envelope on your sheet of paper and make sure that, as far as you can tell, you will have enough at the top, bottom and sides to make flaps that will fold over and easily cover it. For a snug fit, draw a rectangle in this position about ½in (12mm) wider than the card, and ½in (12mm) longer, to mark the front of the envelope.

2. The flaps will need to overlap when they are fixed together. If you are using the plan on this page, flap 'B' should be designed first, and a decision made about how much you want the sides to slope and how close to the top you want its edge to come when it has been folded. Once you have decided this, draw these lines on the envelope paper.

3. Add double-sided adhesive tape close to the side edges of flap 'B', on the surface that will end up inside the envelope, while leaving the outer protective layer in place.

4. Cut around the flap, use something blunt to score along the line that will be the bottom of the finished envelope, then fold the flap up.

5. Measure the maximum distance the inside edge of the adhesive tape extends towards the centre of the envelope, measured from where the edge of the finished envelope will be. Add a ¼in (5mm) to this for good luck, and mark the width of the side flaps, making them this dimension (shown as 'b' on the plan). This will ensure that the adhesive will not attach the flap to the card when it is inside the envelope.

6. Cut, score and fold the side flaps.

7. To construct the envelope, bend the side flaps in first and hold flat, remove the protective strips from the adhesive tape on the bottom flap, then fold the bottom flap on to the side flaps.

8. Shape, score and fold the top flap, making sure that it is going to overlap the bottom flap with enough room to add glue or tape to secure the card inside. You could add a wavy or curved edge and rounded corners if you want a really fancy look.

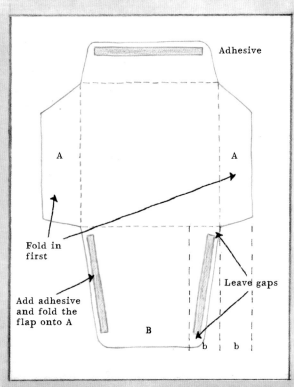

A design for a home-made envelope.

An alternative envelope design

1. First score the bottom flap and fold it up, then add adhesive to the outer surface.

2. Fold the left flap on to the bottom flap and add adhesive to the extra paper, as shown in the diagram and described in the caption (there should be no adhesive to the left of the mid-line). Next, fold the right-hand flap across and attach it.

3. Again, the top flap is designed to overlap the side flaps with room to seal the card inside and cover their sloping edges.

For some envelope proportions, you may find that one design gives less paper waste than the other.

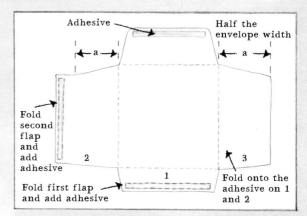

This version has a central line down the back. The right-hand side flap (marked '3' on the plan) is half the width of the envelope (marked 'a' on the left) and the left flap is the same width, plus enough extra paper on the side to add adhesive.

Using Guide Lines for Addresses

When addressing normal white or light-coloured envelopes, try temporarily slipping in a piece of card with guide lines drawn on it, so that you can keep your writing straight and the lines well spaced. For thicker envelopes and to gain most benefit from a light-box, you can photocopy or print guide lines on to acetate sheet. These lines, however, can rub off, so it is advisable to tape a sheet of clear acetate over the top. Of course, you can also use the guide lines on a light-box if the envelopes are thin enough, and then you probably won't need to insert them in the envelope.

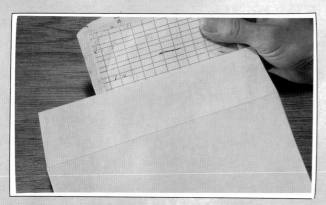

Guide lines on card, inserted into an envelope to aid addressing.

Postal Safety

Both large and extra-small non-standard sizes of envelopes may incur an additional postal charge, and mail delivery personnel may try to fold them if they are large. Adding extra substantial card inside can help protect the contents from being creased but, if your card has decorations that protrude from the edges, or has raised embellishments, remember that most mail travels between rollers in automatic sorting machines. These are good at reducing sea-shells to powder and creating impressions of whole or fragmented buttons in new places.

Depending on the nature of your postal service and what technology is employed at the destination, you may be able to hand a card to an official at a post-office counter and ask for the stamps to be hand-franked with care. If successful, you may avoid having your card's decorative features crushed as well as the inky obliteration of the pictures on the stamps. But you need to ask about their use of rollers at sorting offices – some services may still send the cards through rollers for security checks. If your card is a very special creation, it is safest to mail it in a box, or to hand-deliver it.

PART SIX
gallery of creative designs

The Gallery

The artworks shown on these pages have been created by artists from around the world. It is hoped that they will inspire you to have fun experimenting with new techniques and alphabets and that you will create your own unique layouts and card designs.

Dave Wood, 'Cats': a lively Italic-based script, written with some pen twists.

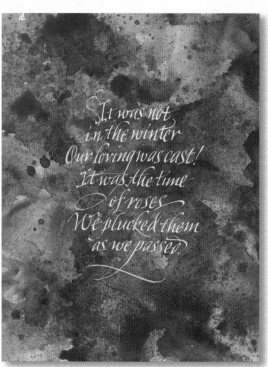

Ginger Meidel, 'Roses': written in Italic with gouache, over splashed watercolour and walnut ink.

Margaret Beech, 'Star light, star bright': lettered using a skeleton Celtic alphabet, with translucent stars.

Dave Wood, 'Spring': resists and pen-drawn letters. Inspiration for a scrapbook page design.

The Shakespeare Family Tree

Elizabeth Hall
1608–1670
m. 1626   m. 1649
Thomas Nash   John Bernard
1575–1635   ?–1674

Thomas Quiney
1620–1639

Richard Quiney
1618–1639

Shakespeare Quiney
1616–1617

Susanna
1583–1649
m. 1607
John Hall
1575–1635

Hamnet
1585–1596

Judith
1585–1662
m. 1616
Thomas Quiney
1589–1652?

William
Shakespeare   m.   Anne
1564–1616   1582   Hathaway
             1556?–1623

Peter Taylor, 'Family Tree': Italic script with cut, torn, punched and shaped paper. An idea for a scrapbook page.

Deirdre Hassed, 'Grazie': Italic-based script with a few pen twists, and gold.

Dave Wood, 'Green Bough': the bird and the Versal lettering are pen drawn.

Angella Peardon, 'Mum': traditional heritage scrapbook layout, with calligraphy.

Peter Lloyd, 'Rainbow envelope': the colours of the pointed Italic letters are those in the stamp.

Margaret Beech, 'Starbook' (back view):
written with a gel pen in skeleton Roman based letters.

Victoria Kibildis, 'Envelope Selection': written in Copperplate calligraphy, both traditional and with variations.

Jean Wilson, 'Envelope': the colours of the Neuland letters, and decorations, match the stamp.

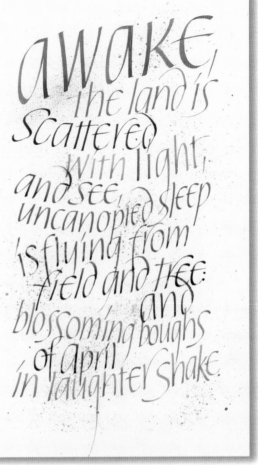

Liz O'Sullivan, 'Awake' from a poem by Robert Bridges: formal Italic lettering using a pen fully loaded with transparent watercolour.

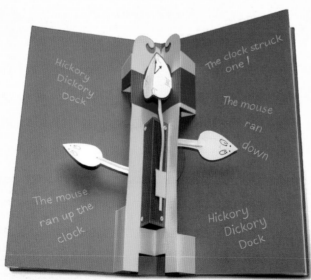

Margaret Beech, 'Hickory Dickory Dock' (pop-up, inspired by Robert Sabuda): small Roman skeleton letters, drawn with coloured pencil.

Glossary

Archival Unlikely to change in colour or change other materials that it contacts over an extremely long period of time.

Bowl The curved and enclosed portion of a letter that is attached to a vertical.

Broad-edged pen A calligraphy pen with a chisel-shaped nib or point with a straight edge that touches the paper.

Counter The fully or partly enclosed space inside a letter.

Cursive Writing with many letters joined without lifting the pen – usually fairly quickly and casually written.

Decorated letter A letter with decorative features that are drawn in addition to the basic shape.

Descender The part of a small letter that extends below the baseline.

Entry stroke A pen movement that slides into the letter before the first proper stroke is made.

Exit stroke The last stroke a pen makes as it completes one letter or leads to drawing the next one.

Flourish A decorative addition to a letter to extend it outside its normal shape.

Gilding Adding gold.

Guard sheet Paper for your hand to rest on that protects the underlying writing sheet from sweat, grease and marks.

Guide line A line that helps to write letters a constant size, on a chosen slope or at a chosen level. It is usually removed from, or not seen on, the finished work.

Hand A style of related letter shapes. Also known as a script or alphabet.

Hue A colour. When white is added, the result is a tint. When black is added, the result is a tone.

Illuminate Create or decorate letters, writing, borders or illustrations with gold or other shiny metals, or with bright colours.

Interlinear The space between lines of writing.

Layout The plan of where writing, pictures and embellishments are to be positioned.

Lightfast Unlikely to fade when exposed to sunlight for an extremely long time.

Monoline A line of a constant thickness.

Permanent ink (e.g. marker pens) Stains paper and is hard to remove. Fade and water resistant – not fade or waterproof.

Pigment The coloured substance that is used to make ink, paint, or an art product.

Platemark An embossed area, usually rectangular, created as a depression in a card or paper surface and into which other layers of paper or card can be adhered, or writing and artwork created.

Reservoir A device attached to a pen nib that allows it to hold more ink.

Roman capitals The kind that were used for the finest carved letters on the most important Roman monuments.

Script A particular writing style or alphabet design. (It can be used to mean a handwriting style – but not in this book.)

Serif A small starting or finishing structure or feature drawn on a letter corner.

Skeleton letter The simplest possible way of drawing a letter to show its proper structure.

Stroke A part of a letter created without lifting the pen from the paper.

Weight of a letter Heavyweight letters are created by using a thick pen to draw letters with comparatively small size. Lightweight letters are created by using a thin pen to draw letters of a comparatively large size.

x-height The height of a small letter 'x' and others like 'a' and 'e' that have no extending ascender or descender limbs.

Further Reading

A few of the books below are out of print, but obtainable from libraries or second-hand book shops, and some overlap with what is provided in this book, or with others on the list. However, they all have something to stimulate the imagination, or they provide extra knowledge, technique instructions, new alphabets, or variations.

MAGAZINES

*Bound and Lettered
and Letter Arts Review*
John Neal Bookseller
www.johnnealbooks.com
Quarterly

BOOKS

ANGEL, Marie
Painting for Calligraphers
Pelham Books 1984
ISBN 9780720714159

BOTTS, Timothy
Door Posts
Tyndale House Publishers
1998
ISBN 9780842305952

BROADBENT, Brenda
Parallel Pen Wizardry
Paper & Ink Arts 2003
www.paperinkarts.com

EBRAHIMI, Hamid Reza
How to Write Copperplate
(supported by YouTube videos)
Hamid Reza Ebrahimi 2010
ISBN 9789640412121

ENGELBRECHT, Lisa
*Modern Calligraphy
& Hand Lettering*
Quarry Books 2010
ISBN 9781592536443

FURBER, Alan
*Layout and Design
for Calligraphers*
Taplinger Publishing 1984
ISBN 9780800845735

GOFFE, Gaynor
Calligraphy Step by Step
(with RAVENSCROFT, Anna)
Collins 1994
ISBN 9780004128030
Also published as
Calligraphy School
Quantum Books 1994
ISBN 9781861607966

HAINES, Susanne
*The Calligrapher's
Project Book*
HarperCollins 1993
ISBN 9780004124834

HARDY WILSON, Diana
*The Encyclopedia of
Calligraphy Techniques*
Search Press 2012
ISBN 9781844488100

Enrich Your Calligraphy
Headline 1997
ISBN 9780747219552

HUFTON, Susan
Step by Step Calligraphy
Weidenfeld & Nicolson
Illustrated 1997
ISBN 9780753802403

LACH, Denise
*Calligraphy: A book of
Contemporary Inspiration*
Thames & Hudson 2009
ISBN 9780500515044

MEHIGAN, Janet
*Mastering the Art
of Calligraphy*
Lorenz Books 2009
ISBN 9780754821786

NISHIMURA,
Margot McIlwain
*Images in the Margins –
The Medieval Imagination*
Getty Publications 2009
ISBN 9780892369829
The British Library 2009
ISBN 9780892369829

NOBLE, Mary and
MEHIGAN, Janet
Calligrapher's Companion
Quantum Books 2007
ISBN 9781845732530

*Calligraphy Alphabets
for Beginners*
Quarto/New Burlington
Books 2008
ISBN 9781845662318

PEARCE, Charles
The Anatomy of Letters
Taplinger Publishing 1986
ISBN 9780800801991

*The Little Manual
of Calligraphy*
HarperCollins 1993
ISBN 9780004118116

SIDAWAY, Ian
Colour Mixing Bible
David and Charles 2004
ISBN 9780715318232

STUDLEY, Vance
Left-Handed Calligraphy
Dover Publications 1991
ISBN 9780486267029

TAYLOR, Peter E.
A Manual of Calligraphy
HarperCollins 1988
ISBN 9780044401254
Also published as
*The Australian Manual
of Calligraphy*
Allen and Unwin 1987
ISBN 9780043000960
Practical Calligraphy
Hinkler Books 2010
ISBN 9781741855647

WATERS, Sheila
Foundations of Calligraphy
John Neal Bookseller 2006
ISBN 9780966530513

WINTERS, Eleanor
*Mastering Copperplate
Calligraphy: A Step-by-Step
Manual*
Dover Publications 2003
ISBN 9780486409511

*Italic and Copperplate
Calligraphy*
Dover Publications 2011
ISBN 9780486477497
(Builds on *Mastering
Copperplate Calligraphy*)

WOOD, Dave
*The Painted Word:
Inspirational Calligraphy*
D. J. Horwood 1999
ISBN 0646363026
Dave Wood Calligraphy Art
Gallery www.davewood.
com.au 1998

Calligraphy Resources

Useful links will be found on the websites of most of these businesses and organizations, as well as a wealth of information, videos, instructions and images of inspirational creations by calligraphers worldwide.

Creative Envelope Design Inspiration

'Mail Art Across the World'
http://maaw.atelier-calligraphie.com/uk/albums.php

The Washington Calligraphers Guild's 'The Graceful Envelope' contest winners in editions of their magazine 'Scripsit', Ed. Lorraine Swerdloff
– available from stores and the Guild
Spring 2009 (Vol.31, No.1)
– Winners 2006, 2007 and 2008
Fall 2005 (Vol.27, No.3)
– Winners 2003, 2440 and 2005
December 2002 (Vol.25, No.3)
– Winners 1995 to 2005

Materials, Equipment and Books

(P) Welcomes personal shoppers.
(M) Mail-order only, selling worldwide.
May set up their store at a conference or event.
(PM) Provides a personal shopper and mail-order service.

N.B. Businesses change their location and services – please make a check prior to a visit.

Australia
Pen-Ultimate Penmanship (PM)
www.penmanship.com.au
Shop 15–17, Level 2, QVB, 455 George Street, Sydney, NSW 2000

The Gold Leaf Factory (M)
www.goldleaf.com.au

Wills Quills (M)
www.willsquills.com.au

Canada
Quietfire Design (M)
www.quietfiredesign.com

UK
Blots Pen & Ink Supplies (M)
www.blotspens.co.uk

Calligraphity (Books) *(M)*
www.calligraphity.com

L. Cornelissen & Son (PM)
www.cornelissen.com
105 Great Russell Street, London WC1B 3RY

Gold Leaf Supplies (M)
www.goldleafsupplies.co.uk

Scribblers (M)
www.scribblers.co.uk

USA
John Neal Bookseller (books and much more)
(*M* – but see the 'about us' link)
www.johnnealbooks.com
1833 Spring Garden Street, First Floor, Greensboro, NC 27403

Paper & Ink Arts (M)
www.paperinkarts.com

Directory

Cynthia Garinther's Calligraphy Directory
(and all paper-crafts)
www.cynscribe.com

Associations, Guides and Societies

This list is not comprehensive – calligraphy associations exist in most countries and regions. Hopefully you will find a link on the website of one of the organizations listed here that will help you to discover a group that meets close to your home (and also follow the 'links' on www.johnnealbooks.com and www.cynscribe.com, too). Some countries have a very large number of state and local organizations, however, many of the bodies below provide so much that is worthwhile for members that people join from around the globe.

Australia

Australian Society of Calligraphers
www.asoc.org.au

Calligraphy Society of Tasmania
www.chooseit.org.au/calligraphy

Calligraphy Society of Victoria
www.calligraphysocietyvictoria.org.au

Canberra Calligraphy Society
www.canberracalligraphysociety.org.au

Coffs Calligraphers
www.coffscalligraphers.com.au

The Calligraphers' Guild of Western Australia
www.calligraphywa.asn.au

Canada

The Calligraphy Society of Ottawa
http://cso.ncf.ca

The Lettering Arts Guild of Red Deer
www.lagrd.ca

Westcoast Calligraphy Society
www.westcoastcalligraphy.com

UK

Calligraphy and Lettering Arts Society
www.clas.co.uk

The Society for Italic Handwriting
www.italic-handwriting.org

The Society of Scribes and Illuminators
www.calligraphyonline.org

USA

The Association for the Calligraphic Arts
www.calligraphicarts.org

Calligraphic Society of Arizona
www.calligraphicsocietyofarizona.org

Calligraphy Centre
www.calligraphycentre.com

Calligraphy Societies of Florida
www.calligraphers.com/florida

Capital City Scribes, Texas
www.ccscribes.com

Chicago Calligraphy Collective
www.chicagocalligraphy.org

Escribiente Calligraphic Society, New Mexico
www.escribiente.org

The Friends of Calligraphy
www.friendsofcalligraphy.org

IAMPETH The International Association of Master Penmen, Engrossers and Teachers of Handwriting
www.iampeth.com

Portland Society for Calligraphy
www.portlandcalligraphy.org

San Antonio Calligraphy Guild
www.sanantoniocalligraphy.com

Society for Calligraphy
www.societyforcalligraphy.com

Society of Scribes
www.societyofscribes.org

Valley Calligraphy Guild, Oregon
www.valleycalligraphyguild.com

The Washington Calligraphers Guild
www.calligraphersguild.org

Acknowledgements

GMC Publications would like to thank Rebecca Mothersole for the original design of this book and Hedda Roennevig for picture research.

Photographic Credits

Page 22 – St Tropez
Top left, map: Hemera Technologies/ Thinkstock © Getty Images
Top right, stamp: Hemera Technologies/ Thinkstock © Getty Images
Top centre, a local man: Marc Veraart
Second row, *left*, houses: Scott Anderson
Second row, *centre*, beach scene: Mark Veerart
Bottom left, suitcase: Thomas Northcut/ Photodisc/Thinkstock
Bottom right, two women: Scott Anderson

Page 51 – Party
James Vaughan/Flickr

Page 63 – Our Great Night Out
Top, AC/DC: Mark/Flickr
Bottom centre, ticket: Michael Karshis
Bottom right, concert: Montecruz Foto

Page 79 – Wedding Day
Top, cake: Donna Barber
Centre, wedding scene: Don O'Brien
Bottom, bride and groom: Herry Lawford

Page 97 – Retirement
Top left, gardening: George Doyle/ Stockbyte/Thinkstock
Top right, beach: Stockbyte/Thinkstock
Second row, *left*, fishing: Stockbyte/Thinkstock
Second row, *right*, safari: Jupiterimages/ Thinkstock © Getty Images
Bottom, cycling: Goodshoot/Thinkstock

Page 117 – Class Reunion
Top right, cassette: Hemera/Thinkstock
Centre, balloons: Stockbyte/Thinkstock
Second row, *left*, boy: Pip R. Lagenta
Second row, *right*, girl: Pip R. Lagenta
Third row, *left*, girl: Pip R. Lagenta
Centre right, class photo: Brian O'Donovan
Bottom, *right*, jam session: Hemera/Thinkstock
Bottom, *left*, boy: Ed Uthman
Bottom, *centre*, boy: Lazzarello
Bottom, *second right*, boy: Paul/Flickr
Bottom, bunting: Comstock/Thinkstock

Page 123 – Spring
Top left, lambs: iStockphoto/ Thinkstock
Top right, bluebells: Hemera/Thinkstock
Bottom right, family: George Doyle/ Thinkstock

Page 126 – Family Picnic
Top left, billycan: Hemera/Thinkstock
Top right, camper van: Ed Yourdon
Bottom left, table: Miguel Pires da Rosa
Bottom right, family meal: Ryan McVay/ Lifesize/Thinkstock

Page 143 – Pure Joy
Top left, play blocks: Hemera/Thinkstock
Top centre, mother and baby: Photodisc/Thinkstock
Top right, mother and baby: Photodisc/ Thinkstock
Centre, rattle: Hemera/ Thinkstock
Bottom left, toy train: Hemera/Thinkstock
Bottom right, teddy bear: iStockphoto/ Thinkstock

Page 176, cutout 'A'
Sara Burgess

Additional photographs by Rebecca Mothersole:

Page 14, *Bottom left*, pen

Page 26, *Bottom right*, butterflies

Page 27, background, and *Centre left*, butterflies

Page 38, *Bottom left*, pen

Page 41, *Bottom right*, pens

Pages 89 and **91**, backgrounds

Page 93, background, and *Bottom right*, card

Page 95, background stars, flowers, words and tint, *Top right*, and *Bottom*, cards

Page 98, background, and *Bottom left*, greeting

Page 99, *Top left*, card

Page 104, *Bottom right*, pen

Page 105, *Top right*, card

Page 116, background, and *Top left*, pen.

Index

To place an order or to request a catalogue, contact:
GMC Publications Ltd.
Castle Place, 166 High Street, Lewes, East Sussex, BN7 1XU, United Kingdom
Tel: +44 (0)1273 488005 www.gmcbooks.com